MW01295907

Retirement

Everything You Need To Know About
Planning For And Living The Retired Life
You've Always Dreamed Of
(A Two Book Bundle)

BOOK 1:
How To Retire
A Practical Guide As You Countdown To
Retirement

BOOK 2:
So You've Retired – what's next?
A Practical Guide For Your Happy Retirement

By

Olivia Greenwell
oliviagreenwell.com

Inspiring Life Design
Unit 16991
PO Box 15113
Birmingham
B2 2NJ
United Kingdom

Would You Like Free Books?

As a publisher, **Inspiring Life Design** is always looking for keen readers who would like to receive free copies of upcoming books. Why do we send out free books? Simply to help with gaining honest book reviews. If you would be interested in joining our advance preview group simply visit:

inspiringlifedesign.com/bookclub

Acknowledgements

I would like to thank the following people for their invaluable support and contribution during the book creation process:

- David Forster – for creative and design input

Contents

BOOK 1:

HOW TO RETIRE

A Practical Guide

As You Countdown To Retirement

Introduction

When I wrote *So You've Retired: A Practical Guide For Your Happy Retirement* my goal was to help people discover what makes them happy and provide useful information on how to enjoy life after retirement. Many of my kind readers wrote to me that they liked my suggestions and that they would also appreciate some guidance on **getting ready to retire**. Investments and other plans to prepare for retirement can be overwhelming and people seem to want to stick their head in the sand when the topic is raised about **how to retire**. I've written this book with the objective of breaking down the intimidating issues and outlining the steps a person needs to take to get ready for their big day.

How To Retire: A Practical Guide As You Countdown To Retirement is a companion book to my first book, however it is inclusive on the subject of **preparing for retirement** and can certainly be appreciated on its own. It should be noted that I am not an accountant, a stock market guru or a lifestyle expert. So what qualifies me to write this book? When I wanted to gain a better understanding of my own retirement situation, I started doing research to find out the steps I should be taking. The financial information was daunting and it took a while to break it down to more simplistic terms. It's not rocket science but it can be confusing and I was able to find a common sense approach and answers to my questions. My desire is to share this information with others, to blaze the trail and make the path a bit easier!

With chapters to help you determine if you can afford to retire, to learn about investments, and how to get the maximum benefits from Social Security, this book will provide valuable information that will simplify the path to financial security. I've added a personal touch to help you figure out the positives and negatives in your life that will help you take stock of your situation and come to some decisions about the best plan for you. And, I've included the outline for a plan with a spreadsheet and other resources for you to utilize in your quest.

Written in a casual style, this book will walk you through the maze of figuring out your assets and liabilities in order to get a handle on your finances, some checklists to aid in discovering your individual needs, and suggestions to help supplement your income after retirement. Sometimes we just need things presented in an easy-breezy style to eliminate the formidable task of preparing ourselves for what can be the most exciting time of our lives – retirement.

I hope you enjoy this book and are able to utilize my suggestions in making your road to retirement as simple and abundant as possible. The rewards you'll receive will be well worth the effort you take now - to ensure many fruitful years ahead. It's never too early or too late to start your countdown to retirement! Ready, set, go!

Chapter 1

So, You're Thinking About Retirement

Your option to retire might be in the immediate future or it could be years away, but it's safe to assume that if you're reading this book then you're **thinking** about retirement. Regardless of your age or your circumstances, it's smart to plan ahead as much as you can. Knowledge is power, as they say, and the more you learn about getting ready for the changes you will encounter and how to plan for retirement, the better prepared you'll be to make a smooth transition when the time arrives.

A growing trend in our society is discovering ways to retire at a young age. This requires discipline and forethought but it is possible! I have some great ideas about how to retire sooner than later that I will share with you in Chapter 9. However, the majority of people considering retiring will be 50 or older, as most people require the extra time to meet the financial demands of leaving a job and the income it provides. Beyond the monetary aspect of being able to afford to retire, there are some situations in which a person might want to retire earlier than they normally would. If a person has some physical or mental health issues or if a family member is in some sort of crisis they would want as much time as possible to take care of those important, time sensitive needs. If someone in an unfortunate situation is faced with the choice of staying on a job longer to get a better pension or spending limited time with their loved ones, I think most people wouldn't be worrying about the money. As Paul Tsongas edifies in his book, *Heading Home,* "No one on his deathbed ever said, 'I wish I had spent more time on my business.'"

Everyone's situation is unique and you might want to ask yourself some questions about **why** you want to retire, to help you determine the best course of action.

- Is it simply what's expected of me due to my age?

- Will I be content when I'm no longer part of a work/social environment?

- Is my job taking a toll on my physical and/or mental health?

- Do I want to start a second career after I retire from my current job?

- Am I looking forward to (or dreading) the free time I will have when I retire?

- What are my expectations/dreams and are they realistic?

I suspect the majority of people who are thinking about retirement are ready to do it whenever they're financially able, but there will be emotional adjustments to be made too and you'll want to prepare for those as well. In addition to learning **how to retire,** I suggest you read my book, *So You've Retired: A Practical Guide for Your Happy Retirement.* It will provide some great insights into the expectations of retirement and ideas to make this new chapter of your life the best it can be.

Even when you are confident that you're ready, willing and able to retire, your hands might be bound by exactly **when** you can achieve that goal. Your specific retirement requirements could be governed by your age, the number of years you've worked for your employer and a variety of other factors.

For example, a person who has been on active duty in the U.S. Army, Navy, Air Force or Marine Corps is able to retire after 20 years, with full benefits regardless of their age. So, anyone who joined the armed forces when they were 20 years old could retire when they're 40! In most cases they don't *have* to retire and can continue serving with the potential for increased retirement benefits. Some military personnel plan to retire as soon as they can, while they're still young enough to begin a second career, or turn a hobby into a part-time job!

The stark realization for most people is that they won't be able to retire before the customary age of 65, after working for 30 or 40 years. By the time most individuals are seriously thinking about retirement, they're in their 50's and they might have neglected to prepare financially or considered other important decisions that might effect if, when, or how they can retire. Anyone considering retirement is faced with the challenge of determining the right balance between working longer to get the maximum financial benefit, or jumping feet first into the retirement pool.

In this day and age, it has become more and more common for a person to move frequently among a variety of jobs throughout one's career and their working-life span. Since many jobs come with some sort of retirement plan or pension, this means there's a chance that a person approaching retirement may have more than one, or indeed multiple, pension pots that will require consolidation. Some corporations offer a "contribution" plan, where both you and your employer contribute to a fund, building up an investment account that will be ready when you reach retirement age. Of course, it's also possible to start saving into your own personal pension plan, with tax breaks for contributions made. I'll explain more about IRAs (Individual Retirement Accounts) in Chapter 5.

Many companies use a "rule" to qualify for retirement benefits, requiring a combination of the number of years a person has worked plus their age. The most common ones are the "rule of 80" and the "rule of 85", which means that once an employee's age and years of service total 80 or 85, the employee is eligible to retire. These "rules" are not mandated by law or by the Internal Revenue Service, but are a feature that many organizations choose to use in their pension plan. You'll need to determine the details of your specific pension plan by reviewing policies and/or talking to your plan administrator. If your plan doesn't use a "rule" then it's likely that you'll have to wait until your full retirement age or take a reduced compensation regardless of how long you've worked for the employer.

It's possible that your work situation is such that you don't have any constraints about **when** you can retire. If you haven't worked for the same company for a number of years then the rule of age plus years worked doesn't pertain to your scenario. When you're self-employed or work as an independent contractor, you have the luxury to decide when you can (and will) retire. You might have other income to provide for your financial security from a spouse/partner's wages, rental property, savings/investments, an IRA (Individual Retirement Account), or a personal pension plan. If you're fiscally prepared then you might be in a situation to take the plunge into retirement whenever you desire!

In Chapter 8 – Make a Plan and Stick To It! – I've created a "countdown to retirement" to help you figure out the details of what to expect and how to be prepared for a successful retirement. If you're the kind of person that wants to go ahead and do that, while this chapter's suggestions are fresh in your mind, go right ahead! If you prefer to wait until you've read everything, it will be waiting for you there.

In the meanwhile, read through the following lists to help you focus on what you're looking forward to in retirement. You'll be able to use your dreams to help keep you motivated to achieving your goals. Go on, write down all the fun stuff you simply can't wait to do when you retire!

MY MOTIVATOR LIST:

What will drive me to save for my Retirement?

Examples:

- *Spend more time with my family and friends*

- *Travel throughout the US in an RV*

- _____

- _____

- _____

- _____

- _____

- _____

THINGS TO CONSIDER WHILE CREATING MY RETIREMENT ACTION PLAN:

I'd like to plan to retire in _____ years.

I have to meet my employer's retirement regulations before I can retire	YES	NO
I am able to retire whenever I want, regardless of the years I've worked or my age	YES	NO
I am physically and mentally capable to continue working for a few more years	YES	NO
I have some personal/health issues and need to retire earlier than I expected	YES	NO
I might enjoy a "semi" retirement and simply decrease my work little by little over the next few years, until I'm ready for a full retirement	YES	NO
I'd like to start a second career after I retire from my current job	YES	NO
I'm prepared not to work at all after I quit my present job	YES	NO
I have a good financial plan	YES	NO
I don't have a financial plan, but I'm ready to learn more about it and get started	YES	NO
I have a spouse/partner who is ready for me to retire and understands my needs and our dreams as a couple	YES	NO
I am excited about not having to go to work and look forward to my newfound freedom	YES	NO
I dread the idea of not having a place to go or a schedule to follow every day	YES	NO
I have a bucket list of things I want to achieve and will write my dreams in the list below	YES	NO

MY BUCKET LIST OF EXCITING THINGS TO ACHIEVE:

Examples:

- *Go skydiving*

- *Take my grandchildren to the country of my ancestors*

- *Write my great American novel*

- _____

- _____

- _____

- _____

- _____

- _____

- _____

- _____

- _____

- _____

- _____

- _____

Chapter 2

What Will Change When You Retire?

Many of us dream of the day we can officially retire, at which time the heavens will open, choirs of angels will sing and the world will be at peace. Well, there are some days like that, and there will be other days when you feel like you've fallen into an episode of the *Twilight Zone*.

When I was working full time as a front desk manager at an upscale hotel I loved my job. Being in the hospitality industry suited my friendly, social personality, which was beneficial in the interaction with our guests. I enjoyed meeting new people every day, solving any problems, and providing the best customer service possible. Working with other like-minded individuals and a national hotel chain that provided quality service and great benefits, I was a happy employee. As much as I loved my job, I was excited when the opportunity to leave presented itself and I was able to transition into semi-retirement where I would be working part-time from the comfort of my home.

When I worked at the hotel I had to get up at a certain time every day (whether I felt like it or not), dress professionally (including high heels), put on makeup and fix my hair, drive 30 miles to work through hectic traffic and stand on my feet (in those painful shoes) for eight hours or longer. Sometimes I had night shifts, which disrupted my sleep pattern and any glimmer of hope for a functional existence was shattered during those periods of nocturnal work. There were days (and nights) that I was often tempted to curse at a demanding customer or kick a lazy co-worker in the butt.

As much as I liked my occupation I went through the week as most people do – dreading Mondays, getting over hump Wednesday and thanking God it was Friday – in addition to working a lot of weekends which are the busiest and most demanding days in the hotel business. Many times, on the way to and from work I sat in my car in gridlocked traffic dreaming of what it would be like to be retired and not have the hassles of commuting to a job that encapsulated 90% of my life.

So, now that I'm retired, do the heavens open and angels sing to me on a daily basis? No, they do not. There are days which are wonderful and much like I dreamed of. I don't have to dress up or drive to a job, and I spend my days doing what I want, not under the thumb of an employer. I've been able to spend more time with my grandchildren, watch sunsets with my sweet dog, and perfect my recipe for whole wheat bread. Along with my newfound freedom, I noticed a significant difference in my bank account. The first month I wasn't working outside my home I saved the $200 I would have spent on gas for my car. I also didn't need a lot of personal maintenance like a hair stylist, professional manicures and clothing upkeep, along with other work related expenses like meals and drinks while I was at work.

However, there were times that I was bored out of my mind and wondered, *what was I thinking when I left my great job?* I missed the social interaction of being around other humans, and the fulfillment I received when I was a part of providing great guest service. My mind craved the problem solving I achieved at work and the duties of filing my monthly reports in a thorough manner. I enjoyed going out for an occasional after work dinner and drinks with my associates. Now, I have to be careful with my budget since I no longer have the option to pick up some overtime work to pay for an unexpected expense.

Everyone has a different scenario. Perhaps your situation is nothing like mine, but there will be similarities of which you should be aware. The main reason I wanted to share my personal experience with you is that I want you to realize that **retirement isn't always what you think it will be**. It's lovely to think of all the positive aspects that retirement will be and push any negative thoughts to the back of your mind. If you embrace the entire picture, plan on the good **and** the bad to happen, you'll be prepared to handle any issues that occur.

It's easy to fall into the trap of planning for retirement as if your circumstances will be the same as they are right now, but a lot could be different. Along with the changes in your behavior, your routines, and your way of life in general, there will most likely be a significant reduction of your income. This will create changes in your lifestyle that you'll need to adjust to, however some of the financial issues will be balanced by reductions in your expenditures, such as the savings in gas that I mentioned earlier.

Think about the conditions in **your** life that will be different when you transition from working full time to retirement or semi-retirement. Will you have children that will still be living at home, or depend on you for expenses, like college? At some point, you might be able to downsize to a smaller home, which will result in lower utility bills. You might even have enough equity in your previous home to add to your retirement fund. Many older adults are drawn to the concept of living in a retirement village or community where they can live in a small home or an apartment, while they enjoy the company of other retirees. Since you no longer have to pay to commute to work, perhaps you have a second car that you can sell. The gas, maintenance and insurance costs will be one less expenditure in your budget and one less thing to worry about as you continue to simplify your life.

Perhaps you're waiting for retirement to move to another location. Sometimes your job demands that you live in one place but when you retire, you have the freedom to move wherever you desire. If you live in an area with harsh winters, you might be dreaming of a home in a location that has warm temperatures year round. Maybe you have children and grandchildren you'd like to live closer to so you can be more involved in their lives. Many foreign countries offer the allure of a beautiful locale and great economic value compared to where a retiree currently lives. It's not always feasible to move to a new place but it is fun to dream of the possibilities, and you might devise a plan to live portions of each year in two different places.

A growing trend for retirees is to purchase a recreational vehicle/caravan either to live in full time, or use for traveling to different locations. Sightseeing and relaxation might be the main goal of having a RV, or there's the option to pick up a seasonal job while enjoying a change of scenery. For instance, in Pigeon Forge, Tennessee there is an annual gathering of people who drive their RVs to a camping site near Dollywood Theme Park and work at the amusement park for a few months, then leave when the busy season has ended. There are similar needs for migrant/traveling workers in the farming and harvesting of a variety of crops throughout the country.

Perhaps you have a tentative plan for where you want to retire but it might be several years away. Your situation could change by the time you're able to retire so have alternative options in case your needs and circumstances turn out to be different than anticipated. Often when you brainstorm about ideas and possibilities some things come up that you never thought of before!

I have a friend who is a single woman reaching retirement age in her teacher's career and she has a younger sister who is a widow and nurse. Neither of them foresee a romantic relationship in their future and the plan for their retirement in about five years is to find a housing situation where they can either live together or get a duplex/condo and be close to each other. They will have their individual independence and yet be able to take care of each other, enjoy the companionship, and share some of their expenses. However, they recently heard about an opportunity to utilize their skills in an orphanage in a foreign country and now they're excited about researching that possibility! One of my favorite quotes is by C. S. Lewis and fits this situation perfectly – "You are never too old to set another goal or to dream a new dream."

Here's a checklist of some things for you to think about "what will change when you retire" based on your individual circumstances and goals:

I plan to stay in my current home when I retire	YES	NO
I'd like to downsize to a smaller home	YES	NO
I'm considering buying a RV and traveling to different areas	YES	NO
I'd like to research retirement communities and see if that appeals to me	YES	NO
I like the idea of utilizing my talents in an opportunity where help is needed, perhaps even in a foreign country	YES	NO
I'd like to semi-retire and work part time from my home	YES	NO
I have a hobby that I want to spend more time on, and it might provide some extra income (see list below)	YES	NO
I have evaluated what expenses will be eliminated when I quit working and I'm factoring that into my retirement budget	YES	NO
I don't want to work anymore when I retire. Ever!	YES	NO
I know I might be bored when I retire, so I am listing below some activities I have planned to keep my mind and body active	YES	NO

HOBBIES TO SPEND TIME ON IN RETIREMENT (could provide extra income):

Examples:

- *Golfing – be an instructor*

- *Pianist – provide lessons*

- *Woodworking – make things to sell at craft shows*

- *Teacher – provide tutoring*

- _____

- _____

- _____

- _____

- _____

- _____

- _____

- _____

- _____

- _____

- _____

- _____

ACTIVITES TO KEEP MY MIND AND BODY HEALTHY:

Examples:

- *Volunteering at a hospital, animal shelter, library, museum, park or for special events in your community*

- *Begin a habit of walking, biking or join a fitness class*

- *Participate in book clubs, political campaigns or charities*

- _____

- _____

- _____

- _____

- _____

- _____

- _____

- _____

- _____

- _____

Chapter 3

Taking Stock of Your Current Situation

As Glinda, the Good Witch of the North says, "It's always best to start at the beginning – and all you do is follow the Yellow Brick Road." Once you make up your mind to start the journey toward your very own Emerald City, the land of retirement, the path becomes clear and you're on your way! As with Dorothy and the friends she meets on the Yellow Brick Road, there will be trials and tribulations along the way, but when you see your efforts paying off and the destination is in sight you will have achieved your goal of getting there.

I always advise people to begin investing and planning for retirement when they are young and create a habit of putting aside a portion of their income. If a person begins saving and investing in their 20's or 30's and increases the percentage each year, they will have a great nest egg accumulated by the time they're ready to retire. However, we all are acutely aware that hindsight is 20/20, so don't beat yourself up about not planning earlier. You can't go back and change the past so just begin where you are **right now**.

Whether you're thinking of retiring in the immediate future or in ten years, knowing where you stand in your current situation will help you figure out what you need to do. When you take stock of your present state of affairs, you are setting the baseline. From this point, you can build on the strengths of your assets - "You had the power all along, my dear." You'll also be able to identify and eliminate the weaknesses - "Be gone, before somebody drops a house on you."

Ok, enough from Glinda. Here's where you begin! Get a notebook or a folder to keep the information you gather about your current situation, and have a place to put the data and ideas you will be collecting as you move through the process of assessing your circumstances. Additionally, you can designate a file on your computer for this information, and/or even create a spreadsheet to keep your figures organized. Don't worry about whether you've got everything perfect – this is just the beginning of pulling together your current facts and brainstorming about possibilities for the future. There's no right or wrong and you don't have to be an accountant, so don't be intimidated about this first step of the journey.

If you are single then you should know the details of your own situation. In most cases where there is more than one person in the household to consider, as a spouse/partner, each of you will want to make an individual accounting and then come together to combine your information, assuming you want to. There could be scenarios where you'd want to keep them separate. There could be situations where ownership of business or property is applicable and the estimated value of those will vary. Just make your best guess about any specific issues that you're uncertain about.

Start by making a list of your **assets**, and estimate the value. Some of these could be anticipated income that might occur later, such as from a death benefit of a parent. Brainstorm for resources that might not be obvious. Your assets will include many of the following:

- Income from your current employment

- Income from alimony or child support

- Home equity

- Other building property or acreage

- Time shares

- Income from rental property

- Business and/or investment in another person's business

- Savings accounts (short term)

- Investments and retirement accounts (long term)

- Stocks and bonds

- Jewelry

- Musical Instruments

- Vehicles

- Boats or other watercraft

- Gold and silver

- Personal items of value, collectible figurines, works of art, antiques, limited editions

- Guns (whether as a collectible or for hunting)

- Sporting equipment

- Mink coats or other valuable clothing and accessories

- Computers and home office equipment

- Game consoles, games, streaming equipment

- Movie and music collection

- Tools and lawn equipment

- Retirement pensions

- Trusts that are payable in installments such as from a lottery win or a structured settlement

- Annuity payments from another person which are held in escrow

- Anticipated benefits from another person, such as being the beneficiary named in a person's life insurance or their will, if they are likely to die before you

This appraisal of your resources will help you recognize your sources of income and estimate your net worth. By making this list, you've identified potential revenue through selling valuable items such as antiques, rare collectibles like baseball cards, and works of art. Be sure you are making the most of your investments by checking your financial account statements and watching for profit and loss. Any investment account that includes stocks and bonds will fluctuate but you might consider changing to a "low risk" group of funds if you are continuing to lose money in a "high risk" fund. If the property you own is in an area where the values are fluctuating, watch the real estate market trends to decide if you want to hold on to it a bit longer, or want to sell it while the market is high. Keep up with gold and silver prices in case you want to cash in your precious metals or jewelry.

Next, you will want to make a list of your **liabilities**, expenditures, and the debts you currently owe. Many of these obligations will be paid off by the time you retire but include them in the list so you can see them and make plans to reduce and eliminate them. Your expenses are likely to include many of these:

- Rent (for those not buying or owning their home)

- Renter's insurance, if applicable

- Mortgage payment (for those purchasing their residence) This often includes property taxes and insurance. If not, or if the home does not have a mortgage, list those items separately

- Other property upkeep, taxes, insurance

- Alimony or child support payments

- Financial assistance given to another person such as an elderly parent

- Utility bills – Electricity, gas, water, sewerage, trash pickup, home phone, internet provider, cable/satellite television

- Additional home expenses – Cell phones and mobile phone service provider, pest control, professional lawn service or cost of maintaining by owner, repairs and replacement costs for interior and exterior of home

- Personal items – Clothing, shoes, hair care, toiletries, laundry and dry cleaning

- Food – Groceries, snacks, meals eaten out

- Pets – Food, veterinarian, grooming, medication

- Healthcare – Monthly premium for health insurance, co-pays and out of pocket costs, prescriptions, vitamins and other health supplements

- Dental – Insurance or out of pocket expenses for cleaning, check-ups, restoration

- Vision – Insurance or out of pocket costs for exams, eye glasses, contact lenses

- Membership fees – Schooling, health club, sporting activities

- Continuing education costs for your profession, a child, or for enrichment

- Student loans

- Donations - Charitable, religious, political, animal rescue or other

- Car loan or debt for other vehicles/watercraft

- Leased vehicle payment

- Bank fees

- Car expenses – Insurance, gas, maintenance

- Other loans through a financial institution or to another person

- Credit cards with balances

- Hobbies – Supplies and equipment for art/crafts and other

- Sports – Equipment and fees

- Entertainment – Movies, music and sporting events, nightclubs

- Holidays and special occasions – Christmas, birthday and wedding gifts

- Vacation expenses – Lodging, travel and food

It's scary how these expenses can really add up, especially if you still have children at home. Keep in mind that these are your liabilities **now**, and many of them will likely not be applicable by the time you retire. Work on paying off any credit cards and student loans because these debts have a way of haunting you forever if you don't take care of them promptly. If you have a home mortgage, check into refinancing the balance to get a lower interest rate and/or new terms that will enable you to pay it off in less time.

Review the expenses on your list. See where you can make some positive changes. When it's time for your insurance renewal, take the time to check other insurance companies for better rates. You could get a lower premium if you take a safe-driver course, or are in a position to adjust your coverage limits or raise your deductible. Banks, gyms, restaurants and many other businesses offer free or reduced services to their "senior" customers. For example, many McDonald's locations offer their 55+ guests a free small coffee. It never hurts to ask! No matter what your age, always be on the lookout for ways you can save using coupons, price matching, discounts and sales.

You might be of the opinion that these little changes won't make a difference and perhaps in your situation, you feel that it's not worth your time and effort. However, many people realize that every penny saved on unnecessary expenses is one more coin to add to their retirement fund and over time, it adds up!

Keep these lists of **assets and liabilities** handy, where you can review and update them often. Making these assessments might have been a bit of a shock to your system, but you'll be surprised how things can change in as little as a few months' time. You've taken stock of your current situation and now you're on your way down the path to retirement. "Close your eyes and tap your heels together three times. And think to yourself, there's no place like home."

Chapter 4

Can You Afford to Retire?

In the previous chapter, you courageously bit the bullet and made lists of your assets and liabilities. The information you documented in black and white might have been pleasantly optimistic, or it could have proved to be terribly discouraging. Regardless of your results, it's always best to know exactly where you stand in order to recognize how to move forward.

Studying your personal facts and figures is the best way to evaluate your current income and expenses, and determine what will be different as you move toward retirement. The number one question for most people is - **can you afford to retire?**

Obviously, the answer to this significant question will be based on your particular circumstances, your requirements for living comfortably, and if you've planned accordingly to achieve your goals. Will you have enough money? Do you think you need more resources, or could you get by with less?

A simple method to estimate what you will need is to use your current annual income and expenses as a base. Look at your lists of assets and liabilities and consider the income and the expenditures you are likely to still have when you retire, and which ones will be out of the picture. If you retired today, do you think you'll need the same amount of money, more money, or less? Using your current income is a good gauge to estimate what you'll need when you retire, depending on your expectations. It's likely that if a person has made up their mind to lower their expenditures and reduce their debt they can live on about half of their current income. So, if your present household income is $40,000 a year, the majority of your debt is eliminated, and your needs are not extravagant, you should be able to live contently on $20,000.

Think about your lifestyle and your current expenses. Many people make a substantial income and still spend more than they earn, and their habits after retirement are not likely to change. If maintaining the same lifestyle after retirement is important to you, then you should anticipate the same expenses of your existing situation, and thus plan to require the same income you have at the present time. There's nothing wrong with those who want to live luxuriously in their golden years, but it will require attentive planning and well informed investment strategies.

If you own your home or have a substantial amount of equity accumulated, you might consider a "Reverse Mortgage" which will allow you to continue living in your home during retirement. With a regular mortgage, you borrow money to purchase a home and make payments to the lender over a period of time – usually from 15 to 30 years. In a reverse mortgage, you obtain a loan against the equity in your home but the lender makes monthly payments to **you**. The funds you receive are usually tax-free and won't affect any Social Security or Medicare benefits. As a rule, you won't have to pay back the money while you still live in your home. When you are deceased, or if you move out of the home then the loan must be repaid so if there's a surviving spouse this could be a problem since the home might need to be sold to repay the funds.

Despite the benefit of additional income there are considerable issues with a reverse mortgage; you must be at least 62 years old, you are still responsible for property taxes and insurance, there are high up-front costs and numerous fees, and interest rates are often higher than traditional mortgages. Critics of reverse mortgages say they are confusing and possibly take advantage of people who don't understand the intricate details. Make sure to do your homework before signing on the dotted line!

As discussed previously, in order to figure out if you can afford to retire you need to consider the issues in your life that might change. There will be expenses that are currently important but might not be in the future, such as transportation costs, a mortgage, etc. On the other hand, there could be items that were not expenses before, but they will be after you retire, such as purchasing a RV, pursuing your dream to travel more often, or engage in a sport or hobby that might be pricey.

Another quick method to estimate your retirement expenses is the application of "the 80% rule." This rule simply approximates that to live comfortably when you retire, you'll need about 80 percent of your current income. For example, if you have an annual income of $40,000, you should be secure after retirement with $32,000 a year.

Once you have a general idea of the target income you want to have when you retire then you can determine how much you need to save to produce an income equal to your specific requirements. Since the rate of inflation and interest rates can vary, stock values fluctuate and other variables occur that affect the outcome, there are no guarantees the method you use will achieve precise results but they are a good gauge.

One method of calculating how much you'll need to save is the "multiple-by-25 rule" which helps an investor determine how much they need to save to produce a specific income. If your post-retirement goal is to have a $40,000 annual income (adjusted for inflation) then you'll need $1 million, since 40,000 times 25 equals 1,000,000. This "rule" reflects the assumption that your funds will generate a minimum 4 percent return on your investment. When the funds mature, you can safely withdraw 4 percent each year without reducing the principal, thus allowing the value of your funds to remain invested indefinitely. Here are some estimates of how long it takes to save

$1 million. This depends on the age you start saving, a monthly payment, an investment return of 10%, and reaching the $1 million goal when you're 60 years old.

- 20 years old - $150 per month

- 30 years old - $450 per month

- 40 years old - $1,250 per month

- 50 years old - $5,000 per month

Yep! That's great news if you're 20 years old but not so wonderful if you're 50+. However, keep in mind that this amount might not be the amount you have to save if you anticipate other retirement income, such as a spouse's earnings, pension plan, IRA, annuity, Social Security, inheritances, and any additional resources. It can be challenging to factor all these variables into one definitive answer to reveal exactly how long it will take to accumulate what you need.

Another aspect to consider is the rate of inflation, and how much your money will actually be worth by the time you retire. Inflation, the rate in which prices rise and fall, is one of the main reasons that people need to save and invest their money. For example, at a 2% rate of inflation a Coca-Cola that is $1 today will increase to $1.02 in a year. At the same rate, the current value of $1000 would decrease, and after ten years it would be worth $817. The US Bureau of Labor Statistics uses the monthly Consumer Price Index to calculate the rate of inflation. These figures are used in an attempt to keep inflation low and the economy at an even keel.

Inflation rates are not always predictable and can fluctuate due to a variety of factors such as oil prices and natural disasters. In 2009 and 2010 the $1.25 trillion dollars in mortgaged backed securities purchased by the federal government turned out to be worthless, and resulted in a deflation rate of -2.10 percent. After Hurricane Katrina in 2005, the inflation rate peaked at 4.69 percent due to over $100 billion dollars' worth of property damage and loss of income for businesses and workers. So, you can see there is a wide variance when it comes to inflation rates. Historically, the average rate of inflation is about 3.40 percent. If you invest your money into an account that pays only 2 percent, when you factor inflation into the calculation (3.40 - 2.00) you will see that you are actually losing money at the rate of 1.4 percent. Well, that's not good! The most logical method to beat inflation is to put your money in an investment that has a return that will average 3.40 percent or higher.

In Chapter 5 I'll discuss some investment ideas to assist you in discovering the best plans to maximize your savings. In Chapter 8 there is a spreadsheet that will provide a lot of useful information and help you determine your specific goals. In Resources (at the end of this book), you will find some links to a few financial sites. You can type in your specific financial data and they will calculate results that are more definitive for your particular retirement income and provide information about the time needed to provide the retirement income you desire.

Take a moment now to fill in your personal information about when you'd like to retire. Then, answer the questions I've added for you to consider as you make decisions about if you can afford to retire, or if you need to prepare for a few more years.

MY CURRENT AGE: _____

**MY IDEAL
RETIREMENT AGE:** _____

**APPROXIMATE NUMBER
OF YEARS TO GO:** _____

(Ideal Retirement Age minus Current Age = Years to Go)

REASON(S) WHY I WOULD LIKE TO MAKE THIS MY RETIREMENT AGE:

What would motivate me to make it sooner than later?

- _____

- _____

- _____

- _____

- _____

- _____

QUESTIONS TO CONSIDER:

- How long will I be physically and mentally capable of working?

- How satisfied am I with my current employment?

- How heavily am I dependent on my monthly income?

- How financially prepared am I?

- Do I plan to work part time after I retire from full time?

- What restrictions might there be on pensions/money available in retirement? (e.g. age I can withdraw without penalty, tax ramifications, etc.)

- When is my partner/spouse planning to retire?

- Will I have any personal commitments requiring retirement sooner rather than later? (e.g. looking after a dependent relative, health issues, etc.)

Although my goal in writing this book is to supply as much DIY information as possible, I would be remiss if I didn't recommend a financial advisor to assist in evaluating your scenario and retirement needs. Most investment companies provide free consultations and if you open an investment account the fees are very reasonable (my IRA account fee is $50 per year), they provide excellent advice according to your individual needs. Another option is hiring a "fee only" financial advisor to act as your fiduciary, they're legally bound to put your best interests first.

The significance of the "can I afford to retire" question is the first step in recognizing your needs for a happy retirement. Yes, I completely understand that trying to figure things out can be overwhelming and intimidating. Don't let the fear of the unknown scare you away from doing what you need to do to achieve a successful retirement evaluation. Despite the daunting task, you're the only person who can make your lists, appraise your circumstances and comprehend your goals for a satisfying retirement. Trust me! When you complete this task you will thank me, and you'll be proud of yourself for taking these steps toward being fully in control of your affairs.

Chapter 5

Investments

An investment can be defined as a person devoting their time, talent, or emotional energy for a purpose. You invest to achieve something, whether it's a moral accomplishment or a financial gain. When you invest your money, you are allocating funds in order to gain profitable returns, such as interest, income, or appreciation in value. I like to think that when you are investing, you're thinking of both definitions – devoting your time and energy in discovering what works best for you **and** making your money earn you the maximum amount of profit.

Obviously, you want to make the most money with the least amount of risk. That's where investing can become tricky and it intimidates good folks that are confused about all the options. It's not hard to understand why some people choose to keep their cash hidden under a mattress and pull it out as they need it. It's certainly less stressful than worrying about losing money in the stock market when you don't have a clue about how that works.

But what about the millions of people who successfully invest in stocks, bonds and other "risky" business? Are they just lucky? Do they have enough money that they don't care if they lose some of it? I sure don't have money to throw away and I doubt you do either!

So, where do you begin understanding investments and how they can benefit you? Do you try to figure it out on your own or find a financial advisor? I'm going to answer these questions and help you recognize that it's not rocket science, and anyone can do it!

First, you should know the difference between the terms APR (Annual Percentage **Rate**) and APY (Annual Percentage **Yield**). When people talk about saving money, they often use APR when referring to the interest rate the bank pays, when it's actually a term that applies to loans or credit cards and the rate the bank charges you for borrowing money. APY applies to deposit accounts and is used to reflect the total amount of interest paid on an account, based on the interest rate and the frequency of compounding.

Ok, what the heck is "compounding"? This is the term used for how financial institutions calculate interest on your deposited money. You might have seen banks advertise "compounded daily" or it could be monthly, or yearly. What this means is that if you keep the money in the account and don't make withdrawals, over a period of years your balance will grow faster because you'll actually be earning interest **on the interest**! Here's an example using an initial deposit of $1000, no other funds deposited and no withdrawals, no bank fees, an APY of 5 percent, and the results after ten years.

- Compounded yearly - $1628.89

- Compounded monthly - $1647.04

- Compounded daily - $1648.66

So, an account that compounds interest daily is the best choice, and monthly is a close second. It might not seem like a huge variance but when you continue to save over the years and your balance gets to $50,000 or $100,000 the difference is substantial. And, when it comes to earning money every bit counts.

Now that we've got these basics established, let's consider the different types of investments. I've divided the following investments into three sections – low-risk, medium-risk and high-risk. Please be aware that some of the investment opportunities I've put in one category can easily overlap into another, depending on the risk factors of the specific investment.

Low-Risk/Conservative Investments

Savings Account

A traditional savings account is probably at the bottom of the list of low-risk investments (besides the under-the-mattress method). Many people might think a savings account is an investment and it is better than nothing, but just barely. Bank APY on savings accounts can be as low as the ridiculous 0.05 percent to an equally absurd 1.10 percent. And, to add insult to injury, some banks charge a monthly fee, which would essentially use up your balance over a period of time. You should never pay a monthly fee for a basic savings account, and you should really be putting your money into an account with a higher APY. That being said, I should stress that every household needs to have a fund (separate from their checking account and higher paying investments) for emergencies or unexpected needs, and a traditional savings account will allow quick access to the money. It's so much nicer to have immediate availability to the $500 you need for an unforeseen car repair than take out a loan or charge it to a credit card.

Money Market Account

Another option to have access to your emergency fund and earn a bit more interest is Money Market accounts, which are sometimes called "interest bearing checking accounts." These accounts usually have a higher APY than a savings account and the convenience of a checking account. There is a limit to the number of withdrawals and there might be a minimum amount for each check you write, to avoid the use of this type of an account in place of a regular checking account.

Certificates of Deposit

An investment possibility in the low-risk range is Certificates of Deposit (CDs), which essentially amounts to giving your financial institution a loan that will be paid back to you with interest in one payment at the end of the period. CDs pay a higher

APY but your funds will be locked in for a designated time, such as 6 months, a year or several years. The APY depends on the amount of time the money is held. A one-year CD will yield about 1-1.5 percent, while a five-year commitment rate is between 1 and 2 percent. It's not a great return, especially for having your money tied up for five years, and if you need to withdraw the funds early, there will be a penalty.

United States Treasury Bills

Another low-risk investment is with U.S. Treasury Bills, Notes, and Bonds (shortened to T-Bills, T-Notes and T-Bonds) which are issued by the US federal government. The purchaser buys a T-Bill (in denominations of $1000) for a discounted price (perhaps $990) and holds it until a maturity date of one year or less, when they receive the full value. T-Notes have the same concept except that they mature in 1-10 years and pay out interest every six months instead of being sold at a discount. T-Bonds are like T-Notes, except they mature in 10-30 years. As with other low-risk investments, treasury notes don't have a high return but they are guaranteed and work for some investors.

Annuities

Annuity investments are contracts with insurance companies, which entail a person contributing a lump sum of money with the goal to produce a stream of income for the future. An "immediate annuity" would begin as soon as you desire while a "deferred annuity" delays the returns for a future period. After-tax annuity contracts are irreversible so people considering this form of investment, albeit low-risk, should evaluate the pros and cons and make sure this is a good investment for their situation. In essence, if you have a pension or plan to draw on Social Security, you already have a fixed annuity in place and your money would be better spent on another form of investment.

Individual Retirement Account

An IRA is a savings method in which a United States taxpayer contributes a certain amount of money each year to an account designated to be drawn upon after they retire. The Traditional IRA allows a person to make contributions and earn interest on a tax-deferred basis until it is withdrawn. Money put in an IRA can be deducted on a person's tax return (up to the yearly limit), which means the person's pre-retirement income will be taxed at a lower rate, and their post-retirement income and tax rate will likely be less too.

A Roth IRA is somewhat different from a Traditional IRA. You fund the account with money you've already paid taxes on and your money, including interest, will be tax-free when you withdraw it after retirement. There are certain conditions that must be met with IRAs and you'll want to check to make sure this is a good investment for you.

An IRA can be set up through a CPA (Certified Public Accountant) or a financial consultant. When you open the account, your advisor will help you determine if you want a Traditional or Roth account, and if you prefer your funds be invested in conservative, moderate or aggressive earning methods. Don't be afraid to ask all the questions you have about the degree to which you can be involved in selecting the various funds and/or changing them periodically. Make sure you understand the financial institution's policies and fees before you commit.

Personally, I did my research and found a great financial advisor who helped me set up the account at my comfortable risk level and I let him do the rest. I watch the account grow from the statements I receive each month and if I have any questions, my representative is just a phone call away.

401(k)

A 401(k) plan is a contribution-based pension account, deducted from a person's paycheck before taxes are withheld. Many employers offer a matching benefit, or a maximum percentage of a person's annual salary. As with the Traditional IRA, the money is tax-deferred until withdrawn after retirement and provides the investor the benefit of being in a lower tax bracket. There is a limit to pre-tax yearly contribution, which as of 2015 is $18,000. If you leave the employment of a company that has matched or contributed to your 401(k) there could be stipulations that will influence the account payout, so be aware of those before you terminate your position.

Since your employer is in charge of the funds you deposit into a 401k account, they (rather than YOU) choose the manner in which your money is invested.

Many organizations offer stock in the company, bonds, other investments, or a combination of methods. Even though you don't have much control over the choice of how your money is invested, the funds are usually governed by a board of directors who must maintain a high level of transparency. If you factor in any matching benefits ($1 per $1 or perhaps up to 10 percent of your annual salary) this is a win-win situation you shouldn't overlook just because you can't pick your own investments.

Medium-Risk/Moderate Investments

Mutual Funds

A mutual fund is a professionally managed investment account that uses money from a pool of investors to purchase and sell securities in bulk on behalf of the client. Each investor will choose if they want to be in a low- to medium-risk fund, or a high-risk bracket. The funds are made up of a variety of stocks, bonds, equity funds and other investments, which are controlled and traded to the public on a daily basis. In comparison to investing in individual stocks, there won't be any crucial fluctuation based on the profit or loss of any single company. Mutual funds are an effective means in which an individual can dabble in the world of stocks and bonds without much concern while a professional is in control. Investment firms charge an annual management fee, which is a reasonable amount, and well worth having someone else micromanage your investments.

Index Funds

Also known as "tracker funds" or "index trackers" these funds are mutual funds that are linked to a broad stock index (such as the Dow Jones Index) rather than being selected as prime investment opportunities by a financial manager. Since an index fund has no active management to buy and sell stock, it's considered a passive investment, and it simply "tracks" other markets like Dow Jones and the S&P 500. Since the returns on a specific investment in an index fund or a mutual fund will be identical, the main drawback with index funds is that an investor would not be alerted to any unexpected opportunities that might occur, which an investment manager would notice. The positive side of index trackers is that there are no management costs (compared to managed funds) and therefore fewer fees to eat away at profits, which can make a significant difference over a number of years.

Bonds

When you invest in bonds, which are issued by corporations and governments, you are basically giving the entity a loan, which they will repay with interest. Bonds have a variety of risk factors depending on the municipality or company that issues them, which will determine the level of risk, and will reflect the potential for a high or low payoff. If a bond issuer claims bankruptcy or defaults on their debts, the investor will lose all of their money, with the exception of any interest that has already been paid.

Stocks

Stocks are "shares" of a company that are similar to the equity of the corporation based on their assets and future earnings. As a business's actual earnings and value increases, the worth of each share of stock increases, and if the earnings decrease the stock value drops. When a company has a profitable year, the shareholders will reap the benefit by now owning a higher valued stock, or they might get dividends (interest payments) reflecting the increased value. Stock prices tend to fluctuate more than other investments like bonds and other funds, so be careful about "playing" the stock market on your own.

High-Risk/Aggressive Investments

The medium-risk investments I talked about can quickly become high-risk if you aren't aware of what you're signing up for. Many stocks are "speculative" with no guarantees, and high-risk bonds might be sketchier than you want to gamble on. Your money manager should always let you know if you're in a high-risk investment and that although you might make a lot of money quickly, you can lose it the same way.

Peer-To-Peer Lending

The P2P Market Place essentially allows investors to "loan" money to other members of the public who wish to borrow money, thus securing a higher return on their investment than many other methods could offer. There are many simple online platforms offering this service, see the link I've provided in the Resources section for some of the best ones. In some ways this is a win-win approach to lending and borrowing, taking the power and fees which banks traditionally impose out of the equation. It works by allowing investors to choose the amount of money to loan and degree of risk they are prepared to take, and then dividing the invested money across multiple different loans in order to reduce the amount of risk. For example, $1,000 could be invested to part-fund 100 different loans of $10 each. Should one of the borrowers default on their loan, only a fraction of the invested amount is affected (in this instance $10). The higher the risk rating for an investment you choose, the higher the risk of more defaults, but the greater (sometimes significantly so) the returns. Although this is still considered a relatively unorthodox method of investment, the returns can be worth the associated risk, and are certainly worth considering when making your investment choices.

Real Estate

Investing in real estate can provide income from using the property as a rental, and if you happen to be "at the right place at the right time" and purchase real estate that turns out to be a gold mine, you'll be smiling all the way to the bank. However, if you plan to invest in real estate you should be very savvy about your acquisitions. Make sure to do your homework regarding the comparative prices of the area, the condition and improvement costs, and the potential development (or decline) of the specific location. You'll need to factor insurance costs for property that has a house or structure on it and taxes on any property you own. What seems like a good deal could turn into a money pit.

Precious Metal

Many people invest in precious metals, usually gold and silver. These assets are easily transported and can always be sold regardless of where you are in the world. Just keep in mind that the prices of gold and silver have a history of great fluctuation and you'll want to consider the price you pay versus the investment potential.

Personal Investments

If you've ever watched the television show *Shark Tank,* you'll understand the important considerations of making a personal investment in another person's company or idea. It takes an expert in business practices to weigh all the factors involved. The risks of starting a business are high, as are the percentages of new companies that fail. I believe the idea of investing in another person's dream is a wonderful concept but it's not a wise choice for investing. When it comes to loaning money to friends or family, I have three words of advice - don't do it. If you just can't say no (which I realize can happen) don't consider it an investment, as the odds are that you'll never get your money back, with or without interest. Before you hand over cash to a friend, write a concise promissory note, with the plan for repayment, and have all parties sign it. Even if it's not notarized, it's still a legal document if you choose to use it in court later if the debt goes unpaid.

Buyer Beware!

Ponzi Schemes

Although you'll never be approached for an investment of this name, you should be aware that there are scams that have taken millions of dollars from people who were promised high returns with low risk, and investors thought they were legitimate funds. Named after con artist Charles Ponzi, the scheme creates returns for older investors by acquiring fresh investors. Similar to a pyramid scheme, they both use new investors' funds to pay the earlier backers and eventually there isn't enough money to go around, and the schemes unravel. As with any investment, a good rule of thumb to follow is – If it seems too good to be true then it probably isn't legitimate! Unfortunately, a person's greed can come into play when they're offered a quick buck and they don't see the drawbacks of a potential fraud. Caveat emptor - let the buyer beware.

Gambling

There are professional gamblers who have made a lot of money from their skills, even though the high rollers know it's all "games of chance." As Kenny Rogers sings, "You've got to know when to hold 'em, know when to fold 'em, know when to walk away, and know when to run." The odds at casinos and other gambling sites (both on premises and online) are never in favor of the gambler. If you enjoy a little recreation, then go and have fun but never think of gambling winnings as a good way to make money.

~~~~~~

The suggestions I've provided in this chapter are not inclusive of all the investment opportunities that might be available to you in your individual circumstances. Even within the suggestions, there are variations and options with different prospects and risk factors. Only you can decide the most comfortable methods to invest your money toward retirement.

Many of these options can be easily accomplished without any assistance from a professional financial advisor. Once you get into the medium-risk options, the aid of a money manager will help you achieve the best results. As I stated in the previous chapter, the yearly fee on a retirement account is minimal compared to the services they provide. While I understand the basics of the different options, I couldn't personally deal with the ins and outs of how to buy, sell or trade stocks and bonds, nor would I want the responsibility.

When you find an investment company and a financial advisor that you trust, let them do what they do best. You can still have as much control as you desire, but you have the option to sit back, relax and let them do all the work. Sure, there will be some ups and downs in your balance over time, but you'll learn to go with the flow. Most often, when I read my monthly retirement account statement I just pat myself on the back and gloat about how smart I am to let some else do all the work and earn money for me.

As you review where you stand in your own situation, make a list of your current investments and savings accounts and consider the following statements.

I am satisfied with the risk level of my current investments	YES	NO
I feel more comfortable making changes now that I have a greater understanding of investments	YES	NO
I don't have an IRA but I'm prepared to start one!	YES	NO
I understand it's important to have a financial advisor and I'm going to find one to help me	YES	NO

Chapter 6

Accentuate the Positive and Eliminate the Negative

The title of this chapter came to mind as I considered alternative ideas for producing income, and plans to eradicate debt as you continue your countdown to retirement. As you approach the goal, it's easy to get overwhelmed about all the changes that will occur. If you have some strategies toward staying focused on the optimistic factors, and reducing the adverse aspects of your pre-retirement situation, it will be much easier to "latch on to the affirmative and don't mess with Mister In-Between."

American lyricist and singer, Johnny Mercer, was the first to record the words he wrote for the song used in the 1944 movie, *Here Come the Waves*. Bing Crosby starred in the film and his performance of "Ac-Cent-Tchu-Ate the Positive" might be the one that people of a "certain age" remember. However, the catchy tune has been recorded by dozens of eclectic recording artists including Paul McCartney, Aretha

Franklin, Al Jarreau, Sam Cooke, Willie Nelson, and Jools Holland with Rumer. It's also been used in television shows like *Quantum Leap, Treme,* and Britain's *Coronation Street* and *Casualty*. In numerous movies, you can hear different renditions of the song, such as Dr. John in *The Mighty Ducks*, and Clint Eastwood singing on the soundtrack of *Midnight in the Garden of Good and Evil.*

Ok, I got sidetracked on all the fun facts about this song. Suffice it to say, the lively melody and optimistic message have universal appeal. On with the subject at hand!

As you evaluate your circumstances, you might see the need to supplement your retirement income. You could continue your current job in a part-time position, or find other employment that has some fun elements, such as a storefront greeter or at an amusement park. If you'd rather keep your source of income closer to home, you can find ways to earn money through a specific talent you possess, or by utilizing a hobby to make and sell items at flea markets and craft fairs. If you enjoy working on the computer and feel comfortable in the world of the wide web, the possibilities are endless!

Accentuate the Positive

Whether you need extra income or you'd just like to keep active during your retirement, it's always a good idea to think of the skills you possess and the things that fulfill your passions in life. If you make a list of your strengths (and even your weaknesses), it will point you in the direction toward an activity that brings you joy. Perhaps you love tennis and you can earn some income by giving private lessons, or you can volunteer your expertise at a youth center. If you're detail oriented and love to read, you can find a job as a proofreader at one of many online freelancer sites such as Upwork, Guru and Fiverr. Maybe you're inspired to write the great novel that's been buzzing around in your head for years. Now that you have the time, why not give it a go?

As I mentioned earlier, I highly recommend you read *So, You've Retired: A Practical Guide for Your Happy Retirement*. I wrote the book with some great ideas for new opportunities that could present themselves in retirement. The chapters include information that will help you discover different ways to embark on new adventures, stay healthy, flex your mind, and embrace your spirituality. The book is a comprehensive guide to assisting you on your quest to learn how to take advantage of your time and talents, from advice on how to get your affairs in order to creating your own bucket list.

Passive or semi-passive income is a term used frequently in recent years that basically refers to money earned with little effort from the recipient. Passive income is becoming more common as advocates enjoy the ability to work from home without a boss hovering over them, and the freedom to work at their own pace. Jobs that can be done from a home computer are appealing; who wouldn't like to stay home and work in their jammies?

Online work is a perfect example of a semi-passive income. There are dozens of Internet sites that connect clients who need specific projects completed, and freelancers who are willing to work on individual assignments. Freelance sites allow a person to create a profile stating their skills, experience, samples of their work and the rate they charge, which is usually negotiable. A client can peruse the profiles, choose from the freelancers that seem best suited for their project and set up an interview to discuss the details. Additionally, freelancers can look at jobs that clients post and "bid" on the job. Many sites monitor the correspondence, work progress, and transfer funds when the job is complete. They take a percentage of the contracted fee, but it's worth it because it would be difficult to connect people without the service.

Freelance sites offer an abundance of categories to narrow your search to the fields that interest you. You can choose from writing, graphic design, translating, legal, sales and marketing, IT and tech support, virtual assistant, and many other specific classifications. Freelancers can find the niche where their skills will be used and appreciated, work as much or as little as they please, and make some revenue doing something they love!

Perhaps you want to start your own website, to sell a product or a service. Maybe you want to start blogging about one of your passions. The main thing you need to be successful in these ventures is **time**, which you will have plenty of when you retire. Always go back to what makes you happy. If you love teaching, create online courses or offer a tutoring service. Readers might enjoy branching out into writing, editing or book publishing. Perhaps you love creating videos and want to put some of them on

YouTube. The opportunities for additional income are limitless. And, if you aren't concerned about supplemental revenue, simply finding activities that will keep your mind active are priceless!

Take time to list your talents, skills, passions and things that make your life meaningful, and brainstorm about related possibilities for the future. I've started the list with a few ideas.

TALENT, SKILLS & PASSIONS TO ACCENTUATE

- *I love animals. I could volunteer at a rescue shelter or become a pet sitter*

- *I play a musical instrument. I can join a local group or give lessons*

- *I like buying and selling on eBay. I can offer to teach my skill to others*

- *I enjoy baseball. I can coach a youth team*

- *I'm a people person. I can join a club, help at the library or visit people at a nursing home*

- _____

- _____

- _____

- _____

- _____

- _____

- _____

- _____

Eliminate the Negative

I believe most people have an image of retirement being a time of peaceful bliss, where we have no stress and do things that make us happy. Perhaps we must bring in a little extra income, but we're going to find a job we can enjoy. Although visions of sitting in a rocking chair with a glass of wine are appealing, we will balance the relaxation with activities to keep us busy – when we **want** to be busy. The most important way we can achieve this goal is to eliminate the negative issues in our lives.

We need to identify and attempt to remove anything in our lives that causes stress or unhappiness. This could be a person, place or thing. Ok, it's not always possible to remove people from our lives, but we can try to repair any rifts that have occurred that are causing tension or discord. Many people wait until it's too late to apologize or mend broken relationships and then have to live with the heartbreak. If you have "toxic" people who bring a bad element into your life, find ways to avoid interaction with them, and if you have to be around them, don't engage beyond being polite.

If you're in a home or live in a city that you don't enjoy, make plans to move when you retire. Sometimes we find ourselves in a place we don't really like due to our employment and after we leave the job, we have the freedom to move to a location we will appreciate. If this is your situation, make preparations to sell your current home by working on any fix-up needs the house might require in order to get the best price. Start looking for a home that will be better suited to your retirement lifestyle. If you hate yard work, you might enjoy condominium living where the lawn maintenance is done for you. Perhaps you want to live in a retirement community where there is a pool, a gym and the opportunity for social activities with other retirees.

The most negative aspect of people's lives is probably uncontrolled debt. It can be a constant source of worry and frustration and every effort should be made to eliminate as much debt as possible from your life. Review your liabilities and make a list of debts you'd like to have paid off before you retire. If possible, consolidate the debts so you only have one payment. If you can't do that, start with the loan or credit card that has the highest APR (interest rate) and pay as much as you can each month. Here's an obvious but not often used tip: You don't have to wait until the payment is due each month! You can pay as often as you like, so if you find yourself with a bit extra money, make additional payments.

Many people find that by setting up an automatic payment it takes the worry out of the situation. You'll never have to pay a late charge and the debt will gradually decrease. While you're employed, you might be able to have a designated percent or specific amount taken out of your salary to be deposited directly to a savings account, or to your retirement fund. You'll never even miss the money because you never had it in your hands!

The most important aspect about reducing debt is not creating more. This might seem like a no-brainer but when credit cards and monthly payment plans are so readily offered and available, it's very tempting. A national furniture store constantly offers, "Take five years to pay with NO interest." Of course, no interest is a huge enticement, but it's still a monthly payment! Think about what you're considering purchasing. Do you really **need** it, or do you just **want** it? There is a big difference!

What about those pesky negative aspects of your life that you'd like to eliminate?

NEGATIVES TO ELIMINATE

- *I need to lose some weight and work on a healthier diet*

- *I will quit smoking. (Doctors are thrilled to offer successful methods!)*

- *There are some toxic people in my life that I will make plans to avoid*

- *I'm going to examine my debts and work diligently to pay them off*

- _____

- _____

- _____

- _____

- _____

- _____

- _____

- _____

Although many aspects of your current lifestyle might not be a "negative" you want to eliminate, consider ways that you can begin a more frugal existence. As you move into retirement, if you make the effort to downsize and reorganize, your new life will be much less stressful and you'll find satisfaction in creating a style of life that is streamlined and efficient. When you retire, will you need two vehicles or a four bedroom home? Is cable/satellite television important? (I saved $100 a month by cancelling my cable service. I get ten local channels with the antenna, spend $10 a month for Netflix and borrow free movies from the library.) Your clothing budget should go down when you aren't working outside your home anymore, and your food expenses will probably decrease too since you won't be tempted to dine out as much.

Look at the expenses in your life and determine any that could be eliminated or downsized. I'm not suggesting that you do without the things that make you happy, but if you don't use a service or it can be economized by switching to a lower plan, put that extra money in your pocket! In fact, start setting aside the money you save and earmark it for a cruise or a vacation that will help you enjoy your retirement even more!

Don't forget another line from the title song that's an excellent message regarding retirement. "You got to spread joy up to the maximum, bring gloom down to the minimum, and have faith or pandemonium's liable to walk upon the scene." As you review the different ways you can accentuate the positive and eliminate the negative in your life, keep a song in your heart and get ready to reap the benefits of your hard work and preparation!

Chapter 7

Getting the Maximum from Social Security

Social Security is the more familiar name for OASDI (Old Age, Survivors, and Disability Insurance) which provides financial security for millions of Americans. Although the focus of this chapter is to discuss Social Security benefits as they relate to retirees, many other people are eligible to receive assistance from this US government program, including disabled persons, and families of disabled, retired, or deceased employees. Funds are collected from individuals through payroll taxes called FICA (Federal Insurance Contributions Act Tax) or SECA (Self Employed Contributions Act Tax). Over 160 million US citizens pay Social Security taxes and approximately 60 million collect monthly benefits. This equates to about one in four families receiving some form of Social Security payment.

The principal element of OASDI is the disbursement of retirement benefits. The program was established to insure that low paid workers did not have to retire without some form of income. If a person doesn't have a job that offers a pension, or if he or she has not been able to save money or invest in a retirement fund, this provides income so a person does not retire in poverty. It's important to note that a person can still draw Social Security benefits even if they are wealthy, have an IRA, investments, or an employer sponsored pension. Social security retirement benefits will be paid for as long as you live, so they deliver protection against the loss or exhaustion of other sources of retirement income.

During a person's employment, the Social Security Administration (SSA) and the Internal Revenue Service (IRS) document their salary and requires taxes to be collected by FICA or SECA. Most people receive a statement once a year showing their lifetime accumulation, but you can go to the SSA website and find your specific contribution if you don't know what it is. While there have been rumors Social Security is "running out of money", the truth is that the Old Age and Survivor's fund is the only Social Security account that collects more money than it pays out.

The amount of an individual's monthly Social Security benefit is dependent upon the amount they've earned and paid FICA taxes on, and the age that the retiree decides to start receiving benefits. A person can draw Social Security when they reach the age of 62, but the benefits will be a reduced amount. Receiving the maximum benefit depends on the person's year of birth. Additionally, if a person delays their retirement beyond the full age, the benefits are increased by a certain percentage according to the year you were born.

For example, say your full retirement age is 66 and according to your lifetime earnings, you'll receive a full benefit of $1000. Using that amount, here's the breakdown according to the age you decide to begin.

- Age 62 - $750

- Age 63 - $800

- Age 64 - $866

- Age 65 - $933

- Age 66 - $1000 (100 percent – the full amount)

- Age 67 - $1080

- Age 68 - $1160

- Age 69 - $1240

- Age 70 - $1320 (132 percent of the full amount!)

So, you **can** begin when you're 62, but as you can see, the benefit increases substantially if you wait. After age 70, the monthly benefit will **not** increase, even if you choose to continue delaying the payment.

You can find your specific information by entering the year of your birth at this link:
https://www.ssa.gov/planners/retire/ageincrease.html

From this page, there are numerous options where you will find charts and valuable information to help you make an informed choice.

Deciding what you should do is contingent upon several factors. There is no right or wrong because it all depends on your individual circumstances and retirement goals. I've made a list of a few considerations that might help you make a decision about the best time to start receiving your Social Security benefits.

- I'm a "bird in the hand" person and I'd rather get a reduced amount several years earlier than waiting to get the full amount

- I have no other source of income and I really need the funds as soon as I can get them

- I don't need the money now but I'll take the payments and invest it

- I'm determined to wait to receive the maximum amount I can get

- I have a spouse and my decision is based on what's best for us as a couple

- I have other sources of income from investments, pension, or my partner's salary

- I plan to keep on working as long as I can. If I start benefits before my full retirement age, any earnings over a certain amount will be withheld

- My health is declining and I'm not sure how long I'll live

- My health is great and my family has history of living into their 90's

- I want to travel and enjoy my retirement as quickly as I can

I must stress that it is crucial to weigh all the factors and consider the direction that's best for you because this decision will affect the monthly benefit you will receive for **the rest of your life.** Once you start drawing Social Security, you can't change your mind. Additionally, your choices might affect the benefits for your survivors after you're deceased, so choose wisely, dear reader.

Regardless of when you decide to start receiving your Social Security benefits, don't forget to sign up for Medicare (government-sponsored medical insurance) **three months before you reach the age of 65**. If you don't enroll when you're first eligible, the benefits can be delayed and you might be subject to a penalty for the length of your coverage.

For more information, check out this site: https://www.ssa.gov/medicare/

When dealing with issues about Social Security you'll hear and read a variety of dubious information. Some people you talk to and/or articles you read offer great advice, while others provide inaccurate data and confuse the facts. I highly recommend that you always check at the **official** Social Security website (*https://www.ssa.gov*) for the most accurate information. You'll find up to date information on the latest COLA (Cost of Living Adjustment), Medicare details, and all the facts you need.

As with most retirement issues, Social Security is not rocket science. It just takes some time to figure out the best plan for you to receive the benefits you've worked for, in a way that works for you. As you continue the countdown to your retirement, learning the facts about Social Security will enable you to get the maximum benefits based on your individual needs and circumstances.

Chapter 8

Make a Plan and Stick to It!

Life marches on whether you're ready or not. You will eventually reach the age when you are willing and able to retire, unless the grim reaper makes you an offer you can't refuse. I think we can agree the second option is much worse than not being prepared, but still...it's a countdown either way.

Whether you get to retirement without any preparation, or you make plans to do everything possible to be financially equipped, it's your call. Nobody's going to hand it to you on a silver platter. It will take perseverance, determination, prioritizing, making a budget and a plan, and sticking to it. It's not difficult – it just requires a commitment to organize a strategy and follow through.

If you're overwhelmed thinking about all the things you need to do to get your specific plans in order, take heart! I'm going to help you get organized! The best part is that once you make your goals and set things in motion, you won't have to worry about it on a daily basis. Of course, you'll need to keep track of your investments, just like you balance your checkbook each month, but if you make good decisions in the beginning, most issues will take care of themselves!

This chapter is a "call to action" for the ideas suggested in this book – basically taking what's been presented in the previous chapters and using it to write your own personal plan of attack. This will help you create an easy to follow blueprint to achieve your retirement goals – physically, financially, and emotionally – to enjoy your golden years to the fullest!

Now it's time for some homework. Get a notebook or papers you can put in a file. The countdown to retirement is on - 3, 2, 1 – blast off!

COUNTDOWN TO RETIREMENT MASTER PLAN

5+ years to go

(as early as you can prior to your desired retirement date)

- Create your Retirement Action Plan

  I've created a spreadsheet which you can use to enter all your numbers and it will show you how much money you need to be saving each year/month to achieve your retirement goal

  o Simply follow this link to access the exclusive Resources area of my website: http://oliviagreenwell.com/resources/htr01cs

  o Open the Google Spreadsheet titled **Retirement Action Plan**

  o Make a copy of the Retirement Action Plan to edit with your own information

  If you dislike using spreadsheets or do not have access to the Internet, then I've also included a copy of the form at the end of this chapter for you to use manually

- Use the spreadsheet to:
  - Calculate the **total savings** you need to accumulate to achieve your desired income for your preferred retirement date

  - Take stock of your current financial situation and work out a plan for how much you need to save regularly (monthly is a good idea) to achieve the total savings you need

- Find a financial advisor (if you don't already have one) to help you set up and manage your savings accounts for retirement, unless you opt to do all the financial management yourself. In Resources, I have provided some links to help you locate a financial advisor

- Consistently achieve the saving rate you have identified

- Get frequent projections for your savings to check you're on target for your desired retirement income and date – adjust your plan/savings rate as necessary

2-4 years to go

- Check your retirement finances

  o What is your income plan for retirement?

  o Consult your financial advisor, check that you're on target

- If you will be eligible for Social Security, think about when might be the right age for you to plan to start receiving your retirement benefits. Factor this into your overall retirement plan

1 year to go

- Continue to check your retirement finances

  o What is your income plan for retirement?

  o Consult your financial advisor, check that you're on target

  o Have you cleared your debt, loans and mortgages if this makes up part of your plan?

- Start to prepare yourself psychologically for retiring

  o Consider refining the list of all the things you're looking forward to doing once you have more time

  o Talk about it with your family and friends so that they know your plans, and you can feel supported by them

- If it's financially viable for you and you/your employer desire it, you may consider a slow ramp-down to retirement by moving to part-time hours

6 months to go

- Give your employer fair warning of your plans to retire

- If your employer provides health insurance, life insurance or other benefits, which might not continue after you retire, start looking for replacement coverage

- Check to see if COBRA might work for you. There are stipulations involved but in many cases you can get health insurance for up to 18 months after you leave your job. COBRA stands for Consolidated Omnibus Budget Reconciliation Act and it's the federal law that provides employees that are no longer working the right to continue coverage in a group health plan. However, it can be expensive since the employer is no longer contributing to the benefit

- If you're eligible for Social Security and/or Medicare, make sure to keep up with those age requirements. (You **must** register for Medicare when you are 3 months away from turning 65 years old, whether you plan to use it or not)

- Check into a life insurance policy with less pay out. Life insurance gets more expensive the older you get but since your family is likely settled by now, it's likely that you don't need as much cover as you had previously

3 months to go

- Consider any aspects of your work that need to be transitioned to another employee

- Ensure your financial advisor is prepped to know your imminent retirement date

- Firm up your leaving date with your employer

- Let family and friends know when you will be retiring

1 month to go

- Start to clear out your workspace/environment and slowly take any of your personal belongings home

- Check in with your employer's Human Resources to make sure everything is lined up for a smooth exit

- Ensure that everything is in place to start receiving income from your retirement savings after your retirement date – catch-up with your financial advisor to be sure

1 week to go

- You may have a retirement celebration to attend during this period

- Ensure you have taken all of your personal items home

- Ensure you have carried out any handover of work

- File any exit papers that your employer requires

- Begin to say any goodbyes around your place of work

- Time to finish off any final pieces of work you've been responsible for

BLASTOFF: R-day!

- Take time to say your final goodbyes to any of your colleagues

- Pass on contact details to colleagues you would like to keep in touch with

- If you have a work email address, set an "out of office" message explaining that you have left the company and provide another contact for people to use

- Inform your friends and family that your big day has arrived. Post a photo on Facebook or send out some emails to let everyone know!

- Hold your head high with a big smile on your face as you leave your place of work for the last time

Post Retirement Day

- Consider checking out my other book *So You've Retired*, which is packed with ideas and information to help you settle into your newly retired life

- Work on writing your Bucket List and start ticking things off

- If you're not getting them already and you're eligible, decide when to start receiving retirement Social Security benefits

- Enjoy yourself!

The realization of your goals will depend solely on how much you're aware of your circumstances (which can fluctuate) and how much you prepare for the future you wish to achieve for a comfortable and enjoyable retirement. Keeping a vigilant watch on your investments, reassessing your situation on a regular basis and continuing to stay organized as you move toward retirement will create an action plan that will make your countdown successful.

Retirement Action Plan

Retirement Action Plan

		INSTRUCTIONS	USING LETTERS
PART ONE - Taking Stock of Current Situation			
Total Debt:	A	Enter your total debt but do not include credit card bills which are already set-up to be paid off monthly in full	
Total Non Retirement Savings:	B	Enter any savings you have in your checking or savings accounts which is not intended for retirement use	
Current Net Position:		Subtract Total Debt from Total Non Retirement Savings	B - A
Total Savings specifically for Retirement:	C	You could consider using some of your savings to pay off debt? Enter the current value of all your pensions, savings and investments which are intended for use in retirement	
PART TWO - Retirement Income Needs			
Income Amount Needed in Retirement: monthly	D	Enter how much income you will need each month once retired	
Annual Income Amount Needed:	E	Multiply the monthly income amount by 12 to get the annual income amount needed	D X 12
PART THREE - Savings Needed to Provide Retirement Income			
Any other anticipated regular income during retirement annually	F	Enter the annual amount of any additional income you will receive during retirement eg anticipated rental income, part time job income etc	
Amount of income needed from retirement savings			
Per Year:	G	Subtract the anticipated additional income from the Annual Income Amount Needed	E - F
Retirement Savings pot needed:	H	Calculate how much money you need to have saved to fund your desired retirement income This uses the 4% rule (multiplying the annual income amount by 25)	G X 25
PART FOUR - Your ACTION PLAN for retirement			
Amount still to be saved:		Subtract your Total Savings for Retirement from the Retirement Savings pot needed to see how much you still need to save in total	H - C
Years Available to save until Retirement:		Enter the number of years remaining until you want to retire	
Anticipated Annual Interest Rate:		Enter the interest rate your investments may be likely to achieve	
Regular amount to be saved to ensure sufficient funds in retirement: per year per month		Use the calculator to work out how much you need to save each year until retirement to fund your retirement pot http://www.calculator.net/retirement-calculator.html	

113

Chapter 9

Sooner Than Later?

Counting down to retirement is a matter of getting all your ducks in a row and keeping them from wandering off. It's easy to let the squirrels (attention distractors) sidetrack us from making plans, sticking to them and waiting years for the payoff. The "ducks" and the "squirrels" remind me of a meme that fits many of us. "I do not have ducks. I do not have a row. I have squirrels and they're at a rave."

You're smart enough to recognize that the planning and sacrifices you make are in anticipation of security for your future, but it can still be frustrating. It's a "hurry up and wait" situation. And, the thought might cross your mind – *What if something happens to me before I'm old enough to retire and I don't live to enjoy the benefits of my hard work and preparation?* There are no guarantees in life and that's why it can be challenging to make plans today to get ready for an unknown tomorrow.

Each individual has their own reasons for the lifestyle they choose. Some people are "workaholics" and wouldn't be happy without a job to go to every day. Many folks thrive on the social atmosphere that a work environment provides. When someone mentions retirement, people with these personalities cringe at the thought. In December 2016, 20 coworkers in a Tennessee auto parts factory won a $421 million lottery, with each bringing home around $20 million. Half of the winners said they planned to continue working! (I do suspect some of them changed their minds later.)

Unfortunately, the odds are that most of us will never have to face that decision. But, what if you could retire sooner than later? Would you really want to wait until you're 60, 65, or 70? If you could figure out a way to retire while you're still young, or at least younger than the traditional retirement age, would you be willing to do what it takes to make that possible?

Well, that's the concept behind FIRE – Financial Independence and Retiring Early. You might have heard of this and wondered if the sacrifices you'd have to make would be greater than the benefits you'd gain.

The payback you receive will depend on your current lifestyle, and the life you want to lead after retirement. Although some people might view the things you need to do to accomplish FIRE as a sacrifice, many will see it as a way to eliminate or reduce unnecessary elements from their lives, and an opportunity to direct their energy toward a happier existence.

Apart from a lottery win or other windfall, you'll have to make some changes in your life to be prepared for FIRE. Increasing the amount of money you save and the rate at which the interest grows is the most important thing you can do to organize an early retirement. There are two ways to be in a position to save a larger percentage of your income - spend less and/or earn more.

Most people are probably already working at a job that brings in the highest potential income. Is it time to ask for a raise? Perhaps you know of a position in your profession that pays more than you're currently making, but you've procrastinated looking into it. Maybe you could find other avenues to produce more income. A second job, either part-time or temporary might be doable. Many retailers need extra help during certain seasons such as Christmas and summer vacation spots, and those jobs would be a short-term commitment, bringing in some extra income. Perhaps you can find a way to make money from home – online freelancer, music lessons, provide laundry or cooking services, yard work, baby sitter, pet sitter, and other previously mentioned suggestions.

It can be challenging to bring in more money, because you don't want to work so hard you don't enjoy life. Instead of earning more, it might be better to focus on spending less because you have more control over what you choose to buy and there is a variety of ways to adjust your expenditures. There are many opportunities to trim down your spending habits, and that's what many are – established routines. It doesn't take much effort to reevaluate your needs versus wants. Prioritize the things that are really important and get rid of the excess. Don't look at reductions to your life as if it's a sacrifice. Now that I'm older and wiser, I look back at some of the things that I wasted so much money on and I want to kick myself! Did I really need a 70" television when a 50" would have been adequate? I can barely bring myself to think about the estimated $10,000 I spent on cigarettes during the ten years I smoked when I was young and stupid.

People waste a lot of money. A lot! Sometimes they think any money left over after living expenses is "free money" and they basically throw it away. Saving that extra money and making good choices will not require you to sacrifice happiness. On the contrary, you'll probably feel much better about your situation! In most instances, saving money on purchases is simply a matter of planning. If you don't make a list and get what you need at the grocery store, it will be more tempting to eat out, which qualifies it as an unnecessary expenditure. You can still enjoy a restaurant now and then but break the cycle of doing it on a regular basis simply because you weren't prepared. Transportation costs are a big budget item and while there's not much you can do about the price of gas, you might be able to use public transportation, car pool, ride a bike or walk. Sure, it's easier to hop in your car and go. That's why you have to think about ways you can change and plan ahead.

OK, once you've discovered ways to make as much income as possible and learn how to trim on your expenditures, now it's time to commit to saving a larger percentage in order to find your way to FIRE. Although investing money is important, you want to concentrate on saving as much as you possibly can. On average Americans save about five percent of their income, probably because it's such an insignificant amount that they don't miss it...it doesn't hurt. It's time to endure a little pain and raise that percentage to ten, and when you get use to ten go to twenty, then thirty, and keep on going as high as you can. Push yourself and make it a personal challenge to save fifty percent of your income. There are people who are living on 20 percent of their income and saving a whopping 80 percent. That's how you can get to an early retirement in about ten years!

On his blog, *Budgets Are Sexy*, author J. Money writes, "...if you want to get serious about reaching financial independence and/or retiring early if you choose to do so, you need to be aware of where you currently stand and what needs to be done in order for you to get there...I never sat down to actually play with the numbers (at least seriously) until today. And boy what a shock that was." In the Resource Page at the end of this book, I've added a link to *Budgets Are*

Sexy where you will find lots of great information to help you determine your early retirement possibilities.

If you really want FIRE, the aggressiveness of your plan will depend on your circumstances. Achieving the goal rests on saving the most you possibly can, as quickly as you can. Obviously, you'll also need to make wise investments so the interest is compounded and the money grows that much faster.

So, is there a secret to investing all this extra money and reaching FIRE? There really isn't a magic formula, unless you're willing to take investment risks that are extremely aggressive. When you are searching for a financial advisor and/or money manager, look for investment companies that can assist you with FIRE, along with traditional investment opportunities.

On the customary road to retirement, you put your plan in gear and meander through the hills and valleys as the years roll by. On the road to FIRE, you're on a super-highway that demands you pay more attention to everything going on around you. It takes an added level of courage and determination to take a different, sometimes frustrating route.

However, as with a country road versus the fast-paced freeway, it might be a bit less comfortable but it will get you there sooner than later. Godspeed!

Conclusion

"Even though the future seems far away, it is actually beginning right now." This profound observation was made by Mattie (Matthew) J. T. Stepanek, a poet, peace activist and motivational speaker. Mattie wrote six books of bestselling poetry, a collection of essays on peace, and country musician Billy Gilman was inspired by Mattie's poems to create his third album, *Music Through Heartsongs: Songs Based on the Poems of Mattie J.T. Stepanek*. In 2004, one year after the release of the recordings, Mattie died of a rare disorder at the tender age of 13.

It's amazing that this young man, who was aware most of his life that he had a terminal illness, was responsive to the fact that the future begins now and he made the most of the time he had on this earth. It's exhilarating to imagine life's potential and especially poignant when that life might be brief. It's humbling to realize that every minute that passes was, just a minute before, the future. And, yet the minute that's gone is now the past, and we can do nothing to change it.

It's important to recognize, no matter where you are on your countdown to retirement, that you don't look back on the past and waste time regretting that you didn't do more to prepare. We all have wished for a time machine on various occasions to go back and do things differently. But, as far as I know, that's not possible so you must accept your present situation and begin wherever you find yourselves. You might be starting your retirement plans on a blank page, be partially prepared, or have all your ducks in a row as you proceed with your countdown.

I've mentioned several times - it's not rocket science - but it can be time consuming and challenging to be aware of all the different avenues on the road to retirement. I've passed along the information I discovered and have tried to explain the process in an easy-to-understand manner. As you've read the chapters and have a better understanding of the planning process, I hope my suggestions have helped you recognize what you need to assure your GPS navigation is on the right path.

Since I'm not an expert, I depend on the knowledge of a financial advisor and I highly recommend that you find one and respect their advice too. I *could* manage my retirement funds, but I am more confident knowing I have a professional looking out for my best interest. I let him do the driving but I'm there to provide the directions (and a little "back seat driver" advice) when needed, to make certain we arrive at our final destination in top form.

While I have made suggestions that cover a wide range of options, I'm aware that the ideas I have provided within this book are not all encompassing. People in extremely high or low income tax brackets might benefit from different opportunities, and they should consult a CPA (Certified Public Accountant) to obtain advice regarding how tax regulations can work to the best advantage. Individuals with income from trust funds or an inheritance will benefit from the advice of an attorney about decisions for their specific circumstances.

What we all can do, regardless of our own situation, is to help young people understand the importance of starting a retirement plan as soon as they begin working full time, even if that's when they're 18 years old. Share this information with your children/grandchildren and encourage them to start saving a percentage of their income from the get-go. If they do, they won't ever miss it! When they understand how interest compounds and how their money will grow, not only from their contributions but also from receiving interest on the interest, they will be more excited about the process. Perhaps you are a math or economics teacher who can explain retirement investments to your students, or you can make a suggestion to your local school board that this information be taught in a life class. Maybe there are financial consultants in your area that would be willing to go to schools or other community outreach venues to explain the extraordinary benefits of planning for retirement. Make the effort to "pay it forward."

As I've stated throughout, each person's situation is unique and should be examined to determine the best plan of action. Excellent ideas for one person might be disastrous for another. Don't feel compelled to follow the same path as a friend, because you might be disappointed when their plan doesn't adapt to your circumstances. When you find a good financial consultant, lay your cards on the table (the good and the bad) because they can provide the best ideas when you are completely honest. Then you can work together to find the plans that are perfect for you.

My passionate wish is that this book has provided some insights that will help you simplify the process and make it less daunting. As you develop your own practical plan toward retirement, you can begin your countdown with self-confidence. Once you take control and get the ball rolling you can rest assured that you've done all you can and then sit back and relax in retirement bliss!

Resources

Chapter 1
So, You're Thinking About Retirement

http://budgeting.thenest.com/rule-85-retirement-30978.html

So You've Retired by Olivia Greenwell

On Kindle:

https://www.amazon.com/So-youve-RETIRED-Practical-Retirement-ebook/dp/B01IO3T3WK

In Paperback:

https://www.amazon.com/So-Youve-Retired-Practical-Retirement/dp/153540809X

On Audible:

https://www.amazon.com/So-Youve-Retired-Practical-Retirement/dp/B01N94JE81

Chapter 2

What Will Change When You Retire?

http://www.cheatsheet.com/money-career/the-biggest-regrets-people-have-about-retirement.html

http://www.aol.com/article/finance/2016/11/10/3-reasons-to-retire-as-early-as-you-can/21603408

http://www.aol.com/article/finance/2016/11/17/26-tips-for-enjoying-retirement-on-a-reduced-income/21608396

Chapter 3
Taking Stock of Your Current Situation

https://www.theseniorlist.com/2016/02/2016-best-list-senior-discounts

http://www.aol.com/article/finance/2016/11/15/this-simple-chart-can-show-you-how-close-you-are-to-early-retire/21606691

http://www.thepennyhoarder.com

Chapter 4
Can You Afford to Retire?

http://www.dummies.com/personal-finance/real-estate/mortgages/the-pros-and-cons-of-a-reverse-mortgage

http://www.moolanomy.com/327/a-closer-look-at-the-80-retirement-rule/

https://en.wikipedia.org/wiki/Reverse_mortgage

Calculators:

http://www.kiplinger.com/tool/retirement/T047-S001-retirement-savings-calculator-how-much-money-do-i/index.php

http://www.bankrate.com/calculators/savings/saving-goals-calculator.aspx

https://www.edwardjones.com/preparing-for-your-future/calculators-checklists/calculators/retirement-savings-calculator.html

Chapter 5
Investments

http://www.forbes.com/sites/laurashin/2013/05/09/10-questions-to-ask-when-choosing-a-financial-advisor

http://money.usnews.com/money/personal-finance/financial-advisors/articles/2014/02/26/how-to-find-a-financial-advisor-if-youre-not-rich

http://www.forbes.com/sites/feeonlyplanner/2013/04/24/5-ways-to-invest-your-money

http://www.aol.com/article/finance/2016/11/16/60-of-americans-invest-too-conservatively-for-retirement-study/21607592/

http://www.investopedia.com/terms/p/ponzischeme.asp

http://monevator.com

Chapter 6
Accentuate the Positive Eliminate the Negative

https://en.wikipedia.org/wiki/Ac-Cent-Tchu-Ate_the_Positive

Ways to earn passive or nearly passive income:

http://www.smartpassiveincome.com

http://fourhourworkweek.com

http://liberate.life

So You've Retired by Olivia Greenwell

On Kindle:

https://www.amazon.com/So-youve-RETIRED-Practical-Retirement-ebook/dp/B01IO3T3WK

In Paperback:

https://www.amazon.com/So-Youve-Retired-Practical-Retirement/dp/153540809X

On Audible:

https://www.amazon.com/So-Youve-Retired-Practical-Retirement/dp/B01N94JE81

Living a frugal lifestyle:

http://www.frugalwoods.com

http://www.theminimalists.com

Chapter 7
Getting the Maximum from Social Security

https://www.ssa.gov

http://money.usnews.com/money/blogs/on-retirement/2013/08/02/7-rules-of-thumb-for-retirement-planning

Chapter 8 Make a Plan and Stick To It

http://www.mrmoneymustache.com

http://earlyretirementextreme.com

https://www.medicare.gov/supplement-other-insurance/how-medicare-works-with-other-insurance/who-pays-first/cobra-7-facts.html

https://www.healthcare.gov/unemployed/cobra-coverage

Retirement Action Planner:

http://oliviagreenwell.com/resources/htro1cs

Chapter 9
Sooner Than Later

http://jmoney.biz

http://www.budgetsaresexy.com

Examples of people who have already achieved financial independence/retirement quickly:

http://www.gocurrycracker.com

http://www.1500days.com

http://financiallyfreebyforty.blogspot.co.uk

Examples of people sharing their path to retirement journey:

http://organisedredhead.blogspot.co.uk

http://www.donebyforty.com

http://thefirestarter.co.uk

http://quietlysaving.co.uk

http://www.earlyretirementguy.com

http://www.fourpillarfreedom.com

Conclusion

https://en.wikipedia.org/wiki/Mattie_Stepanek

https://en.wikipedia.org/wiki/Music_Through_Heartsongs:_Songs_Based_on_the_Poems_of_Mattie_J.T._Stepanek

BOOK 2:

SO YOU'VE RETIRED – WHAT'S NEXT?

A Practical Guide

For Your Happy Retirement

Introduction

As you embark on the exciting journey into retirement, you will experience a transition that will be both thrilling and terrifying. The evolution from a busy job to a life of leisure seems like a no-brainer, however if you don't have a few basic concepts of how to coordinate your time and the activities that will bring you happiness, you might find yourself bored stiff and frustrated.

There's no doubt that you've been looking forward to this stage of your life, where you can put the stress of a career behind you and move ahead to enjoying the fruits of your labor. This book will help you navigate the uncharted territory, from practical advice on how to get your affairs in order, to creating your very own bucket list of all the things you've always wanted to do.

As enjoyable as retirement can be, if you begin by creating a foundation of "cleaning house" and making certain your wishes will be respected by having important documents organized, then you can proceed with your adventures without worrying about technicalities. You will find practical advice on what's important and what's not, and how to decide what works best for YOU.

I've got you covered when it comes to discovering what interests YOU, and will provide ideas to enhance your retirement years. Within these pages, you will find suggestions on a variety of topics, such as fun ways to travel, how to stay fit, methods to flex your mind, and learning to embrace what spirituality means to you. In addition to the suggestions provided, you'll find links and ideas for further research in the Resources at the end of the book. The options are as limited as your imagination!

This book is a comprehensive guide to assisting you on your quest to learn how to take advantage of your time and talents. My wish is that, as you pursue the peace and contentment of your retirement, I have played a small role in helping you discover what makes YOU happy, and how to enjoy your life to the fullest.

Chapter 1
So You're Retired

Congratulations! You've probably worked most of your life to reach the coveted milestone known as retirement, which, up to now, has always been a faint light at the end of a long tunnel. The passageway you've traveled has finally come to the end, and the previously dim goal has turned into a gloriously bright beacon, shining directly on YOU. Attaining this elusive moment will likely initiate celebrations of various proportions, gifts, tears, and cheers all around. The delight emanating from a new retiree has been known to inspire embarrassingly ridiculous happy dances (which you hope no one is quick enough to record on video and put online.) As joyous as this stage of life should be, it can also strike terror in the heart of the strongest warrior. At some point it's likely the idea will cross your mind that retirement implies you've been put out to pasture, and you have nothing to do for the next thirty-odd years.

To say that retirement is an adjustment is an understatement. Everything changes and your world may spin out of control if you don't come up with a plan for this new phase of your life. It doesn't require an outline for each moment of your day, as your previous employment might have dictated, but acknowledging the modifications your new life demands will allow you to make the most of your time, energy... and sanity!

Recognizing there will be alterations in your life is important. Anticipating and planning for changes will assist you in a successful transition. Keep a list of potential issues, especially those that pertain to your specific circumstances. Concerns can be addressed more efficiently when they are written down in black and white. You might consider beginning a journal, or a diary or a notebook to record your thoughts and ideas. (I'm not suggesting that you might be forgetful at this stage of your life. Ok, I *am* saying that. Make a list. Write things down.)

When you are suddenly available 24/7, you can spend more time with your family and friends. This is good. You've no doubt looked forward to having more free time and there are endless opportunities available to you and your loved ones. You might be the last of a group of friends to retire and they've been anxiously waiting for you to get involved in adventures you can all enjoy together. Your spouse might be thrilled to have you home and has her "honey-do" list ready for you to begin.

Newfound freedom has its downside too. Be cognizant of the fact that those around you might not have the luxury to come and go as easily as you, now that you are retired. Perhaps they don't have the funds to participate in your adventures, and they misinterpret your excitement as being boastful. Family and friends that aren't used to having you involved will need as much time to adjust as you do. Your spouse, not being used to having you around, might resent your constant presence at home. Recognize the potential of this happening in advance, and make a plan to avoid too much togetherness for a while. Communication is vital. Talk to your loved ones and discuss expectations about what will occur with your relationships when you retire.

Financial considerations are crucial for your retirement years. There is often a substantial reduction of income when a person leaves their job, and if they have not diligently saved their pennies over the years, they must adjust their new lifestyle to their retirement income, or lack thereof in some cases. Hopefully, you've made some preparation with an IRA, a pension plan, or other method to supplement your income and that will not be a worry for you. Life goes on, even on a limited budget and in subsequent chapters there will be ideas for enrichment and activities that don't cost a dime.

Perhaps you intend to work part-time, either at a job, or from your home. There are many "freelance" or self-employment opportunities to use your talents and interests to provide additional revenue. A few ideas are listed below.

- Pet sitting can be extremely lucrative and enjoyable if you like animals. You can provide this service in your home, preferably with a fenced yard. In some instances, you might be able to combine pet sitting and home sitting for people who like someone to occupy their home while they're away.

- Use your skills to freelance online. Clients seek assistance in hundreds of categories such as writing projects, accounting, translation, photography, art, computer related jobs, and many other services. Freelance websites connect freelancers with clients, and they protect both parties.

- An experienced "handyman" can provide an economical option to people who just need a small job done and don't need a big contractor. Painting, cleaning and other minor jobs don't require many supplies, and your "elbow grease" can pay off handsomely.

- Gardening and landscaping opportunities are great for retirees who enjoy being outside and exercising their "green thumb." You might find there are people who are willing to pay for simply pulling weeds, so they can start their planting in clean soil.

- Check into becoming an Uber driver, if you enjoy driving and meeting new people.

- If you are physically able to keep up with a child, babysitting a few days a week can provide a nice income. Additionally, there are elderly folks who need assistance with cooking, cleaning, transportation or even a companion to read to them.

These are just a few ideas about ways to earn extra income without a huge commitment of time or resources. Don't forget to write a simple contract to confirm the terms of a job, and check your insurance policies to be sure you're covered for jobs in your home or vehicle.

The most significant aspect of retirement is the golden opportunity to focus on **what is most important at this stage of your life**. As we mature, learn life's lessons, and glean a wealth of experiences, we reach an understanding about what's essential to our physical, mental and spiritual well-being...and what's not. Retirement provides the chance to do the things we *want* to do, not the things we *have* to do. We've reached a point where we've earned the right to do whatever makes us happy. The goal of this book is to inspire people, provide useful information, and encourage retirees to discover avenues where they can enjoy their lives to the fullest. With awareness and a little preparation, you'll be ready to embark on this new journey. Welcome to the best time of your life!

Chapter 2
What's Next

You're officially retired and your opportunities are limitless! In truth, this realization could be a bit overwhelming and the adjustments daunting. Never fear! I'm here to present some ideas to help you transition from a working stiff to a life of leisure.

You're perfectly entitled to spend a week or two lolling about and literally doing nothing, if that makes you happy. After the dust settles and the excitement of celebrating your retirement wanes, it's a perfect opportunity to contemplate your situation and make some plans for the future.

The changes in a recently retired person's life will vary according to what they've been accustomed to doing. There will simply be more time to do the things they love! (And, if you aren't quite sure *what* you love, I'm going to help you find out.) If a person has always kept busy, the freedom to participate in their chosen activity will be a welcome respite. Golfers will enjoy more tee time. Shoppers will find exciting places to look for bargains. Hikers will seek out challenging trails. Pool loungers will have plenty of time to fine-tune their suntan.

An important step in paving the path toward a worry-free retirement is to take advantage of the freedom from obligations and get your house in order, both literally and figuratively. This is a perfect time to downsize. Clear away the clutter of unused possessions you've collected over a lifetime, and you'll sweep the cobwebs of disorganization out of your life. This gives you the pleasure of starting fresh, with nothing holding you back from moving forward.

Set a date and begin sorting through your home, attic, garage and storage areas. Depending on your hoarder status, this might take some time, but if you'll do a bit each day, it will soon be finished. You might be able to enlist help from your family and friends, if you entice them by saying it's a party (things are much easier after a few bottles of beer and some pizza). On a more serious note, this process will make life much easier, not only for YOU, but also for your family who will otherwise be forced to sort through your things after your death. Yea, you don't want that. Here are the four areas you need to consider when organizing your belongings.

- **Throw away.** At one time, you might have thought you could *never* throw away your child's kindergarten scribbles, but now they're disintegrated and it's time to dispose of them. Most people only need to keep tax records/receipts for three years, so throw away those boxes from the past forty years. (You might need a shredder, or a big bon fire will work, especially if you're utilizing the party sham.) Items that are broken, melted, sticky, crumbling, rotted, greasy, mildewed, moth eaten, mice nibbled, unrecognizable, and/or beyond repair need to go in this pile. No, you can't fix it, and it will make some lovely flames.
- **Give away.** These items are not trash, but things you don't need or want. They might have a bit of redeeming value, but not enough to try to sell. Clothes that don't fit (or you haven't worn in ten years) are welcome contributions to thrift stores. Old towels and blankets are treasured by animal rescue organizations. Get

plastic bins for items you want to pass along to your children, grandchildren or close friends. They might appreciate enjoying these things **now** rather than inheriting them after you pass on. Baby blankets (of now grown children), nick-knacks, Christmas decorations, artwork, tools, jewelry, and mementoes from family trips are just a few of the personal items you can pass on for others to enjoy. Sentimental items can be hard to part with, but knowing someone else will appreciate and value them will ease the pain.

- **Sell.** Items of value can be sold through a variety of methods, and with a bit of time and effort you'll accrue a nice fund for a vacation or other expenses. EBay is a popular choice for collectors' items and valuables. Designer clothes, handbags and shoes can be taken to a consignment store for the best price. Furniture, vehicles, musical instruments and large items are best advertised in a local newspaper or a "Thrifty Nickle" type magazine. Craigslist is widely used and often successful, but it has drawbacks so be cautious when posting and communicating! Household gadgets, kitchen do-dads, trinkets, books, toys and other small, inexpensive items sell quickly at yard sales and flea markets. Whatever does not sell, box it up and take it to a thrift store. Some charities offer free pick-up and you can schedule them to come at the end of your sale. Don't even think about saving it!

- **Keep.** Trust me; there will be plenty left over after you've gone through the previous three steps. If you take time to organize the stuff you've kept, it will help your life run much smoother. Put photos in albums or sort them into small boxes by the year they were taken. Heirloom quilts, tablecloths, and other cloth items should be stored in an airtight container. Display your mementos and souvenirs in a curio cabinet so that you can enjoy them, rather than have them stored in a box under your bed. (Yea, I know about the under-the-bed boxes. Things go in there and might not be found until twenty years later.) Organize your garage or tool shed where you can quickly locate what you need when you need it.

You will be surprised how much lighter (physically **and** emotionally) you will feel when you've accomplished clearing away unwanted things and putting the rest of your possessions in order. Now, there's one other significant issue of organization to address, and then you'll be free of my nagging and can move on to the fun stuff.

It's imperative that you review your important papers, make sure they are up to date, and placed in a location that your next of kin or designated representative can find them. Here is a list of the vital information others might need. You may not need an attorney to create some of these documents, however you must refer to your state's requirements to make certain they are written, signed and notarized in a legally binding manner.

- **Health Insurance Information.** If you become ill or incapacitated, someone should be able to locate your health insurance information and speak to health providers about your treatment.

- **Living Will.** In the event you are near death and unable to communicate, this document states your desires regarding extending extraordinary measures to keep you alive.

- **Power of Attorney.** This is a written authorization, giving your permission to allow another person to act on your behalf. You can make it as general or as specific as you want.

- **Will.** This document provides your direction in appointing someone to manage your estate and/or the distribution of your property after your death. If you do not wish for your will to be read before your death, make certain you provide the name of the attorney or law office that will have the will on file.

- **Directive for possessions not covered in a Will.** Most attorneys won't want to detail everything you own, and who you want to have it after your death. You can type a list, have it signed, notarized and added as an amendment to your will. It's also a good idea to discuss these wishes with your executor, or the person who will manage your estate.

- **Pets.** Your pet will be confused and lost without you if you reach a point that you can no longer care for them, for whatever reason.

Arrange for a friend or family member to adopt your pet and provide a good home.

- **Funeral Arrangements.** Many people arrange their final wishes and, in some cases, pay for their funeral expenses in advance. This might include your selection of a casket and burial plot, or the process of cremation, if that is your preference. Leave this information where it can be promptly located.

- **Life Insurance.** Keep policies where your loved ones can find them and submit a claim. A recent report has shown that billions (yes, that's a B) of dollars of life insurance funds have been unclaimed because no one ever filed for them. They probably didn't even know there was a policy. If you have a life insurance policy, make sure your beneficiaries are able to collect the money you want them to have!

Many of these suggestions seem like common sense, but millions of people die without having a will or other directions to ease the burden of loved ones who are left to sort out the aftermath. Do yourself and your family a great favor by having these documents in order and easy to locate when needed.

Although the suggestions in this chapter might appear droll, they are important factors in your transition. Once your house and essential documents are in order, you will be able to enjoy the rest of your life without worrying about these issues. Now, let's move on to more exciting retirement ideas!

Chapter 3
Home Is Where The Heart Is

As you ease into the transition of your new lifestyle, consider if you are happy in your current home, or if the idea of relocating to another place appeals to you. If you are "getting your house in order" as discussed in the previous chapter, you might feel like you've gained confidence about making additional changes to create a worry-free retirement.

One or two people don't necessarily need a four-bedroom house with a huge yard, and the idea of a smaller home and garden (or no yard to mow!) might be just what you need. Moving is not fun, by any stretch of the imagination, but the benefits it could provide might be well worth the effort. Make an assessment of your current situation and consider the following questions.

- Is your house too big? Is it too small? Think of who will be living there, your specific needs, and if you can manage the basic upkeep.
- Is your current home in need of major repairs?

- Do you have the space for things you want, such as a garden, a pool or hot tub, or a fenced yard for pets?
- Do you anticipate the need for a home with easy access and wheelchair accommodations? Will you be able to maneuver stairs for the rest of your life?
- Are your family and friends within a reasonable distance?
- Do you like your neighbors and the neighborhood?
- Do you like the city, state, and country where you live? Is it safe? Is the cost of living reasonable? Do you like the climate?
- Would you consider moving to a foreign country? If not, perhaps a second vacation home is an option.
- Are there opportunities for the activities you love, such as parks, theater, sports events, restaurants, or beaches?
- Are there good hospitals and medical options available?

After reviewing this list, you might realize you're already in your perfect home! You are completely happy where you live and would never consider moving. Staying in an established location allows you to keep all the people you love, the places you enjoy, and the things you've grown accustomed to, and this is priceless! Perhaps there are some improvements, alterations, or redecorating you've wanted, but you've never had the time. Now that you're retired and had the opportunity to de-clutter, you can enjoy the rediscovered space in your home and make it look awesome. You can turn that extra bedroom into a workout room or a quiet reading area. You might want to add a patio, with a grill, and a hot tub! A new coat of paint in the kitchen, installing ceiling fans, or replacing carpet with wood flooring are projects that bring a fresh look to your home. The possibilities are endless! Even small changes will enhance the home you've lovingly built up over the years.

If your current living situation is not ideal, not "fixable," or you decide you just want to move and start fresh somewhere else, use the list above to help you decide what will work best for your specific needs, desires, and circumstances.

There's a new trend you might consider, which is most commonly referred to as "tiny houses". These very small homes are compact, efficient, and provide the obvious benefits of downsizing to the max. The economic tiny house can be built on a plot of land, or there are many that are constructed on a trailer base, allowing for moving to different locations. Tiny homes are certainly not for everyone, but they do appeal to many people and it might be an option to consider.

Another idea is to think about whether a retirement village would suit your needs. These communities vary in the options they offer. Some provide private homes or apartments for people who are self-sufficient, and some have transitional benefits that include caregivers and medical assistance for those who require help. Many of these retirement communities have amenities such as a clubhouse, pool, gym, transportation, cafeteria, and 24 hour security. Once again, this is not for everyone, but it could be an option to consider, especially if you are single and would appreciate the care and companionship these villages offer.

These are just a few suggestions to help you decide if you want to move, or if you *need* to move in order to create the lifestyle you desire. Sometimes it all boils down to what is most important to you, and that might not be 100 percent clear at this point in your life. Give it some thought, and don't be afraid to act if you decide on an option that will satisfy your needs and aspirations.

It's likely that you have grandchildren at this stage of your life, and spoiling them will occupy a lot of your newfound free time. Before you retired, you might not have been as close to your family as you would have liked. It's never too late to make up for the time lost. Talk to your family and let them know you want to spend time with them. It doesn't always have to be something magnanimous. Small things such as a walk in the park, or going to get ice cream can be more memorable than a big commitment, such as a week's vacation together. (A week? Yikes! Are we having fun yet?)

Often, the decision to be close to where your children and grandchildren live is a huge factor in relocating. Even if you don't currently live close to them, you can allot times throughout the year to visit them, go on adventures together, and enjoy the quality time you will spend with them. Seek activities that are age appropriate for the little ones. Schedule dates, as a group with the whole gang, and individually, one on one. This will reinforce the bond with your loved ones and provide some great memories!

Besides your family, another great joy of retirement is being able to spend more time with your friends. Now that you're free, you can plan adventures together! Cruises, road trips, or enjoying a favorite restaurant together is a great way to strengthen your friendships. You can open your home and invite people in, to enjoy a variety of activities such as dinner parties, game nights, watching a movie, book clubs, wine tasting, or simply provide a relaxing place to hang out.

You might find that you no longer have things in common with some friends. After you retire, you won't see your previous co-workers, clients, staff, and other people you were involved with on a daily basis. Time you spent working together with these associates, might have been the only mutual interest, despite the fact that you got along well. There could be a bit of jealousy or resentment that you're gone, off having fun, and they're still stuck at the job. If you have a truly good friend from work, this transition will not affect your relationship. For those that withdraw, don't take it personally. Even if you aren't close pals any longer, it's always nice to have acquaintances that you enjoyed for a season.

As you develop your interests, you will discover new friends that share your current retirement status, and/or the enjoyment of activities you have in common. For example, perhaps you've decided to volunteer at your public library. As you work with the staff and the patrons who frequent the library, you'll find people that share a mutual interest. Maybe you want to join a book club, or start one of your own. The love of reading brings people together in a cerebral way, and the casual atmosphere of a book club meeting lends itself to finding friends.

Many sports activities require team interaction, and being part of a group can be fun. If you're trying out a new venture, don't feel locked into it if it doesn't feel right. It's nice to try new things, but learn to trust your instinct about whether you should continue, or chalk it up as a learning experience and try something else. Friends often come along when you least suspect it, so don't feel forced to find new friends. Cherish the ones you have. Quality is always better than quantity.

As you move forward in your retirement, you will face many decisions. Some of them will be easy choices and others will be formidable. Weigh your options and go with your gut feeling. That always works best. Remember, home truly is where your heart is. You can't go wrong when you follow your heart!

Chapter 4
Embark on a New Adventure

Whether you have grand post-retirement plans, or you're just going with the flow and taking one day at a time, you are on the path of a new journey. If you don't have a specific strategy for what you want to do, just enjoy this new phase of your life until something strikes your fancy. Follow the advice of the popular expression - Don't worry. Be Happy.

The first three chapters of this book provided some guidance for recognizing the changes and the adjustments that will need to be made when you retire. Suggestions were given for adapting to your new life through "getting your house in order," making sure your important documents are up to date, and deciding where you want to live. Although certainly not mandatory, these ideas are intended to establish a firm foundation, to create an environment that is worry-free. Once this is accomplished and your "bases are covered," you will feel more confident about embarking on new adventures.

Many people have discovered that their newfound freedom allows time to travel and explore areas they couldn't before retirement. Travel expands the mind and makes you look at the world in a different way. Journey to unexplored areas of the US and foreign countries, learn more about other cultures, try unique foods, and bask in the awesome powerful feeling of going somewhere you've never been before. Make a list of the places, and transportation methods you enjoy, and don't be afraid to try new options. Here is a list of some travel options to consider.

- **Bicycle.** Discover parks, trails and other interesting routes. This simple, inexpensive transportation can be done alone, or with a group, and bike excursions can be as long or as brief as you like.

- **Motorcycle.** People who enjoy riding motorcycles can travel alone, or enjoy the comradery of a group, on a bike tour, or in a "poker run." As with bicycling, you can feel the wind in your hair for a few hours or several days.

- **Personal car, truck or SUV.** It's convenient when you can drive your own vehicle and be able to proceed at your leisure. Road trips are infamous for the ability to stop to see unique sites along your way. They can produce memories that last a lifetime, although with small children, they can be challenging! (Are we there yet?) You could even consider buying a vintage car, which is not only fun to travel around in, but would qualify for joining a specialty vehicles owner's club. They offer opportunities for social meets, displaying unique cars, and other events centered on the common interest.

- **Tour Bus.** Many companies, both domestically and internationally, offer tours via bus. This method of travel can be slow, but it provides many benefits you wouldn't have on faster transport. You'll have the ability to see the scenery that you would miss on an airplane, plus the friendly atmosphere of being with a group of like-minded people. Often led by a seasoned tour guide, bus tours are great for single travelers too, because they are instantly part of a team.

- **Train.** Trains are fun and you can enjoy the passing scenery at a faster pace than a bus or personal vehicle. Unfortunately, train routes in the US are somewhat limited, but in Europe and other countries, this is an excellent mode of transportation. For the ultimate in luxury you could take a trip on the legendary Orient Express, with luxurious sleeper cabins and fine dining.

- **Recreational Vehicle.** Many retirees love the idea of traveling in an RV. They have the freedom to go where they want, when they want, and without concern for hotel reservations or restaurant stops. The camping experience is memorable as you meet other travelers on the same wave length. Often RVs are a means to live in another area for a period of time, such as "snowbirds" who like to reside in a warmer climate during winter.

- **Airplane.** This is obviously the fastest mode of transportation if you only want to get from point A to point B. When making reservations, find flights that allow lots of time between multiple legs, and enjoy the variety of the different airports along your journey.

- **Cruise Ship.** An adventure on a cruise ship provides transportation to a destination (often multiple ports) but it also provides almost everything else you need for a trip – a place to sleep, food, entertainment, scenery, and plenty of people to meet. An "all-inclusive" cruise is relatively worry-free and reasonably priced, when you consider what you get for the fare. There are actually people who have chosen to make a cruise ship their retirement home. They travel year round, with all their requirements met, often for a cost cheaper than other retirement options!

Contemplate some ideas about where you'd like to go, and what you'd like to see and experience. Often your destination will dictate the means of travel that best suits the journey. For instance, if you want to visit the Grand Canyon, a personal vehicle, RV, or tour bus would be the best options for viewing various locations around this huge tourist site. You can get to Bermuda by plane, but a cruise ship will casually take you there and allow plenty of time for you to explore the island. A visit to the United Kingdom would require a flight from the US, but after you arrive, you will have many travel options, including the underground "tube" when you're in London. (Mind the Gap!)

As you plan your adventures, you can solicit the help of a travel agent who will offer advice on many issues. Virgin travelers or people uncomfortable making their own plans should seek the assistance of a travel agency. (There is usually no charge to the consumer, because the agents are paid by the company to book reservations.)

Don't forget that you will need a passport for traveling outside the US. For first time applicants this can take up to six weeks so plan accordingly! Watch the expiration date of a current passport and start the renewal process when it's six months from being expired. Additionally, a travel visa and/or immunizations are required to enter some countries. Research your destination before you make reservations to ensure a smooth adventure. As of 2016, cruise ships **disembarking and returning** to a US port do not require a passport. A birth certificate is acceptable. However, if you are visiting a foreign country during the cruise and need to depart in the event of an emergency, you will have difficulties trying to exit the country via airplane without a passport. It's simply a good idea to have a valid passport!

If you are a single traveler, without a spouse or travel companion, there are great options for tours with a group, who will embrace a solo tourist. If "double occupancy" is required, tour group representatives can help match you with another single traveler. Some cruise ships offer rooms for single occupants, including a lounge area to encourage the solo travelers to mingle!

Many people enjoy planning their own trips. They search the internet for information about destinations, reservations, car rentals, cruises, and just about anything you can imagine regarding traveling. **Always** check for "senior" discounts and last minute deals. (One of the benefits of being retired is the freedom to take advantage of situations like a half-price cruise that leaves in one week.) Some cruise lines offer a price guarantee, and they will match a lower price found on another website. However, some of these offers require certain stipulations, so read the fine print. Always read the fine print!

Don't think that some of the adventures I've suggested have to be long, expensive or complicated. Take a mid-week break and drive a few hours to an area you love and spend one night in an inexpensive hotel. (Many hotels and attractions have lower prices Monday – Thursday.) Take an afternoon to enjoy a museum or science center. Join your grandchildren in the park for a bike ride and picnic. Here's a fun fact: The US National Park Service offers US citizens or permanent residents age 62 and over a **lifetime** Senior Pass for a one-time cost of $10. Previously known as the Golden Age Passport, the pass admits the senior and the passengers in the vehicle! How's that for a freebie!

Envision the things that you love, the things that bring you joy, and the things you always wanted to do. Some people find it helps to brainstorm and make a list of possibilities, to get their thoughts written down for later review. Develop a hobby or activity that you already know you enjoy, but that you previously didn't have time to indulge. Do some investigating and see what it takes to accomplish a dream you've had. Perhaps you always felt artistic. Take a painting, photography or writing class and see if it sparks more interest, or if you can put it behind you without any desire to continue. Learn a new language or how to play a musical instrument, talk to your friends and family about their interests and get together for activities you can enjoy as a group.

The adventure possibilities are virtually endless. It all depends on what you want to do. Don't feel like you have to be doing something fantastic every minute of the day, but make plans to have a bit of fun several times each week. You might think that some of these options are beyond your budget, but you will find most of them very economical. By putting away a few dollars here and there, you'll soon be on your way to an exciting adventure!

Chapter 5

Eat to Live ~ Live to Eat

As you venture into your retirement years, maintaining a healthy body is imperative! You need to be in good physical condition in order to do all the things you want to do. Excess weight and being out of shape can prevent you from enjoying your life to the fullest.

It can be challenging to change a lifetime of poor eating habits and a sedentary existence. Perhaps your pre-retirement job kept you deskbound, or your lunch consisted of a soda and a bag of M & M's. Maybe swinging by the coffee shop for caffeine and do-nuts on your way to work was an essential part of your morning routine. Many work settings indulge in social activities such as potluck meals, birthday parties, and after-work visits to a sports bar for munchies and adult beverages. Ok, it was fun, but in many instances, there might have been a sense of duty to participate. Now that you're retired, you can leave those obligations behind you. This is the perfect opportunity to make a reckoning of unhealthy behaviors, and strive toward better choices.

Diet is a four-letter word, and I mean that in the nastiest sort of way. Just the mention of the word sends fear and loathing into the boldest humans. Diets are not fun, they are restrictive and tortuous, and nobody wants to be around folks who are dieting. When people go on a diet, they turn into grouchy, pathetic zombies, stumbling around in a food-induced craze. Trust me. I speak from experience as a dieter and as a spectator of others dieting attempts. I think I can safely say that nobody likes a diet.

That being said (and made explicitly clear) eating healthy food and learning to control portions will help you lose weight and make you feel better. If you need some help recognizing accurate portions, check out the "portion plate" and other convenient measuring devices that make it easy to determine the correct serving size. Simply avoiding usage of the "d" word will work wonders on your attitude and help you make changes to your eating habits without feeling deprived. Think about managing what you eat from an optimistic view, rather than the negativity a strict diet often elicits.

Most adults recognize foods that are good for you and those that are not so good. I won't even describe them as "bad" because the idea behind what I suggest is that even foods that are considered evil can be eaten in moderation. Take time to become informed about the truth in food production, labeling, and frequent false or misleading information. A good example of this is the butter vs. margarine argument. Butter is high in cholesterol, saturated fat and calories and yet it's a natural food made from real milk. Margarine is an artificial "spread" that is made from vegetable oil and often contains trans fat (the bad kind). Studies have shown that margarine increases heart disease risk, while butter may be nonthreatening. And yet, the use of butter is considered "bad" and the use of margarine is acceptable. It's important to do your homework and research the foods that you love and learn the truth about whether they are harmful, or healthy in moderation.

If you are insecure about your understanding of food, seek information online or take a nutrition class to help you become more confident. Some health insurance policies cover nutrition counseling, and free information can be obtained at your local library and health department. It's important to view your new eating decisions in a fun, optimistic fashion. Look at it as another adventure - an opportunity to learn, and even make new friends in a cooking class or at the farmer's market checking out the fresh veggies.

Many restaurants offer "heart healthy" options so you can still enjoy eating out with your friends and family. A salad is always a good choice but keep in mind that "low-fat" salad dressings often have four times the calories of regular dressing. If you haven't eaten at a favorite place in years and you just can't resist the hot wings, fettuccini alfredo, or that yummy dessert, then go for it! Splurging occasionally isn't the end of the world. Divide large servings in half and take some home for lunch the next day. If you are on a cruise, resisting many of the exciting menu items can be impossible. A saint could not fight the urge to try the chocolate molten cake, and I'm not even going to pretend it's healthy.

Take advantage of senior discounts offered at many restaurants and fast food locations. Many places don't advertise their discount so be sure to ask! Don't be hesitant to use a 2-for-1 coupon, or arrive before the crowds for an "early bird" special. When eating at a buffet, take small portions of what you really want, and only go back if you are truly hungry. It's tempting to feel like you need to get your money's worth, but consider how much better you'll feel walking away satisfied and not stuffed.

Sharing food is a primal activity. It's an opportunity to expand your senses, and share your home and your table with friends and family. Visit a vineyard and participate in wine tastings. Enjoy themed dinner parties, neighborhood bonfires where you'll eat hotdogs and s'mores, and church potlucks. Cook with your grandchildren and don't be afraid to get messy. Volunteer at a soup kitchen, not only to "give back" but also to help you realize and appreciate what you have in your life.

You must "eat to live." The choice of what you eat, how you approach the idea of being healthy, and the joy that can come from eating and sharing food and drink with others is powerful. It's a basic function of life but it can be an extraordinary delight. "Live to eat" doesn't mean you become a glutton. It means you finally realize there can be joy in experimenting with new tastes, flavors and different ways to enjoy food. You don't have to eat huge amounts to appreciate the dish.

There is no firm answer to each person's situation. If you have **any** medical issues you should **always** consult with your physician before making changes to what you eat. Individual health conditions, prescription drugs and other factors might prevent you from the ideas I've suggested. Perhaps the best advice I can give is, simply be aware of your eating habits and aim toward making them as healthy as possible.

Chapter 6
Exercise and Stay Fit

Part of being healthy is making good choices about the foods you eat. An equally important aspect of getting and staying fit is to remain active. Becoming a couch potato might have been on your retirement to-do list, but after a few weeks I'm certain you're ready to check that off and move on. So now, if your muscles aren't withered from inactivity, get off the couch and do something!

At the beginning of each year, fitness gyms are swarming with people who've made a New Year's resolution to get in shape. By February, the crowds have disappeared and only a few faithful remain. Let me be clear. There is nothing wrong with going to a gym! Contrary to my aversion to regimented diets, gyms, hospital sponsored fitness centers and organizations like the YMCA offer some great benefits. Just make sure your attraction to a gym is realistic and you're sure about it before making a long-term commitment.

Fitness establishments provide more exercise equipment than anyone could want and fitness instructors to help you figure out how to operate the complicated machines. Many places offer classes in a variety of areas such as nutrition instruction, yoga, spin racing, weight lifting, and programs like Zumba, kickboxing and self-defense. Some fitness establishments have a swimming pool for water aerobics, lessons and even free swim periods. A few fitness centers include luxury options such as saunas, steam rooms, tanning beds, juice bars, personal trainers, and massage services!

Joining a gym or other fitness program can be a great way to get started, or to continue staying in good physical condition. It feels nice to treat yourself to this specialized service, and to have access to professional equipment and knowledgeable instructors. The group atmosphere can be encouraging as you see others working toward similar goals. Some people might find themselves intimidated by other people, you know, those slim, tan, beautiful, muscular ones that barely break a sweat. Thankfully, "no judgement" policies are gaining popularity among gyms to discourage the idea of comparing yourself to others.

A negative aspect of a gym or fitness center is the cost. Some establishments require a membership fee or a long-term commitment, which they usually want paid in full before you even begin. What happens if you don't like it? Check the refund policy before you sign a contract! Many gyms charge extra for personal instruction, specific classes and those luxury services. There are reasonably priced gym services that are basic, if you don't care about all the "bells and whistles." Check with your local gym to see if they offer a tiered pricing structure, where it's less expensive to go at off-peak hours, which is perfect for a retiree's flexible schedule! It's up to each person to make the decision if the benefits of going to a gym supersede the cost.

Another consideration about joining a gym is that you have to get up and GO to the gym. Yea, bummer. It's amazing how easy it is to talk yourself out of dressing in your workout gear, with the burning question - do I shower before so I'll look good, knowing I'm going to get sweaty and need to shower after? Then, you have to get in your car and drive to the gym in the heat, wind, rain, snow or whatever the weather decides to be that day. Of course, I'm being factious. The point I'm trying to make is that going to a gym has its advantages, but don't overlook the downside. There are a variety of other activities that you can do beyond gym life, and most of them don't cost money!

Walking is probably one of the best exercises you can do at your own convenience, and it's free! Use your phone or other listening device to enjoy music while you walk, but always be aware of your surroundings to be safe. Check your phone for apps that will help you keep track of your progress, provide maps for routes to explore, and even monitor your heart rate. Many people prefer to walk in quiet, and meditate, pray or think about their day. Follow a route around your neighborhood, walk in a park, on the beach, or use a local school's football field track. (FYI – four times around equals one mile.) Many communities have mile markers on bridges, scenic routes and even inside shopping malls. If you want to walk in the woods or other isolated area, find a buddy to join you. For safety's sake, if you walk alone, take a walking stick, whistle, pepper-spray (for wild animals/crazy people), a cell phone and plenty of water in case you lose your way. Brisk walking is refreshing and it gives you a chance to enjoy nature and clear your mind.

Many people who enjoy walking will move on to jogging and maybe even train to run a marathon. For some, a marathon is a possibility to consider and an admirable accomplishment for those who train and become successful participants. Plus, there are some really cool medals that you get, along with the bragging rights that you actually ran a marathon! If a full marathon (approximately 42k/26 miles) is too big a leap, you could try a 5k, 10k or a half-marathon. There are races that offer fun elements such as bubbles, rainbow colors, hot chocolate, rock 'n roll, and even marathons for Disney lovers. The American Heart Association and other organizations have events that raise money for worthwhile causes through walks and runs. Check online to discover endless opportunities for events that match your interests, and will provide fun while helping you stay fit!

Golfers around the world would be furious if I didn't recommend their sport as a great form of exercise, and it is. Golf provides a day out in nature, being active, and a chance to be with friends who also enjoy the sport. The same can be said for tennis, community baseball and basketball teams, swimming, skating, volleyball, croquet, or just about any activity you have fun doing. Don't feel like you always have to be with a group of other seniors. Being around young people helps keep us on our toes, and we might even learn something from the whippersnappers!

If you'd like to combine staying fit with doing a good deed, consider volunteering at a hospital, museum, an animal shelter, or other prospects that interest you. You'll stay busy walking and running errands, and get to be around people of like minds. If you enjoy animals, there is always a need for people to walk, bathe and even foster a pet until it finds its forever home. Owning your own pet can be a great experience too! You might find you want to get involved in professional dog shows, either as a participant or as a spectator. Even if your pet is a Heinz 57 mutt, you'll enjoy the companionship of your furry friend, and daily walks will be good for both of you.

Geocaching is an increasingly popular activity for people of all ages. It's a modern day game of hide-and-seek, using GPS and navigational methods to locate hidden treasures. Many people join geocaching clubs and participate in team searches. It's a great activity to get some exercise, enjoy nature and utilize your sleuthing skills.

If dancing tickles your fancy, take lessons and learn to trip the light fantastic. There are numerous options depending on what interests you and a companion, if you want to learn as a couple. Ballroom dancing is always popular, as is square dancing and country style line dancing. In addition to the great exercise it provides, learning to belly dance or hula dance allows you to embrace and appreciate a different culture. If you're a little shy or concerned about what your two left feet will do, buy or rent an instructional DVD and learn the basics at home.

There are many opportunities within your daily routine to help you stay fit. When you go get your mail, walk around the block. Do some sit-ups while you're watching TV. Always take stairs in lieu of an elevator. Stretch your muscles while you're cooking. It's not rocket science - just move your booty whenever you have a minute or two.

DVDs and videos on YouTube are a great way to explore endless possibilities for exercise and enrichment without much investment. The benefit of viewing them in the privacy of your living room allows you to discover what truly interests you. Don't be afraid to step out of your comfort zone and try something new. You can always say you tried it, and it wasn't your cup of tea. Think about some of these suggestions and brainstorm for some of your own ideas as you seek your niche in the world of staying in shape. As always, do the things you like and the things that bring you joy. You'll feel better, look better and be more content with your life when you stay fit!

Chapter 7
Flex Your Mind

It's important to keep your body in shape and it's equally vital to exercise your mind. Seek activities that will expand your knowledge and have fun at the same time. Despite the advice of a well-known adage, you **can** teach an old dog new tricks, and learning new things will magnify your world!

Reading is a wonderful opportunity to explore new ideas, and whether you prefer fiction or non-fiction, you can drift off into an adventure in your mind. Reach outside your normal reading preferences and learn about things that aren't familiar, to stretch your imagination. Most communities have wonderful libraries where you can find a plethora of options besides books. Some libraries might charge a small fee for a membership, but most have no charge, unless you keep loaned items over the due date.

At your library, you will often discover free classes or lectures on a variety of subjects, along with computers, eBooks, books on CD, movies, and music videos and CDs. Log in to your library online and search the library's selection, put items on hold, and renew checkouts. If you want something that is not available at your local library, they have access to an interlibrary loan service, which can get an item from another system. Volunteering at a library is a great way to help the staff, promote the activities, assist with used book sales, and get to know likeminded folks.

Additional ideas to keep your mind active are brainteasers like crosswords, word search puzzles, and Sudoku, which can be played by yourself. Board games such as chess, backgammon, Scrabble, Monopoly, picture puzzles, and a horde of other offerings will provide challenges as well as fun. Many games involve team players and test your skills in drawing (Pictionary), trivia (Trivial Pursuit), strategy (Apples to Apples), coordination (Twister), and brain skills (Cranium.) There are the "luck of the dice" games like Sorry, and Candy Land, which you can enjoy with your young grandchildren. Card tournaments that include Bridge, Pinochle, Hearts and Poker encourage competition, team play and even a bit of gambling, if you desire. Whether you like silly party games, seriously competitive choices or children's games, don't be afraid to branch out and learn some up-to-date alternatives. Although playing these games in "real life" allows you to be involved with other people in a social setting, many are also available to play on your phone, iPad or computer.

You might be in a situation that you'd like to continue your education, either toward a degree or simply for personal enrichment. Inquire at your local college, trade school or university, as many provide tuition-free classes to seniors. Community colleges and civil organizations provide free or low cost classes on many subjects. For courses that involve making an item, such as art projects, sewing, or gardening, there will probably be a fee for materials. You can learn a foreign language (from beginner to advanced), home decorating, creative writing, computer programs, and many other stimulating choices.

Many businesses offer free lessons in their stores, to help customers learn a new craft, and of course buy the supplies from them! Fabric stores, sewing centers and craft suppliers offer a variety of learning experiences, such as floral arrangement, children's crafts and picture framing. Home building stores have free classes on such topics as how to install wood flooring, caulk a bathtub, and other home improvements. Garden centers and nurseries will offer advice on the best plants to grow in the region where you live. Think of the different ways you can learn more about a subject that interests you, and you'll most likely find a class to help you learn more about it.

You might be in a situation that you are an expert in a skill and would like to offer your services to teach a class, or mentor a person in need of your expertise and knowledge. If you enjoy working with children, you might consider being a tutor at a local public school. Libraries, schools, hospitals and daycare centers appreciate volunteers who will come and simply read to children. Some people, whose first language is not English, need a person to help them learn to read, write and speak their new language. This would be an extremely rewarding opportunity for retirees looking for a way to make a difference in their community.

In discussing methods to keep your mind active, I would be remiss in not addressing the issue of Alzheimer's disease. There are ongoing advances in diagnosing and finding a cure for this debilitating illness. Exercising the mind through brain strengthening activities has not been a proven remedy against the disease, but it certainly can't hurt. Inspiring stories, such as that of recording artist Glen Campbell, indicate that the effects of Alzheimer's can be delayed. With assistance from his family, Glen was able to continue to tour and perform years longer than expected. Simply knowing that you should do everything you can to keep your mind strong is reason enough to flex your brain on a daily basis.

Chapter 8
Take Advantage of Technology

Learning to keep up with the latest information about computers and mobile phones can be daunting for those who are "technology challenged." We love our comfort zone, and often the newfangled gadgets don't make sense to us older folks. You must take into account that it was just over twenty years ago that cellular phones became widely used. I barely had my flip phone figured out and along comes the iPhone, android phone, and other James Bond devices I can't even comprehend. When my flip phone died last year, I went to my cell service store and, at the badgering of my adult children, purchased an iPhone. I asked the representative for an instruction book and she looked at me as if I had two heads, and finally told me I can find out how to operate it online. Right. So, I did what every self-respecting, technology ignoramus does and asked my grandchildren.

I am among many that don't really care about the most up to date apps and social network opportunities. I know people who still have a landline phone, and refuse to get a cell phone, so I consider myself in the middle of the dilemma. However, I recognize that there are many people who **love** to learn the newest technology. I bow to their fearlessness. The same can be said for the computer wizards, who understand how to use a computer to its maximum potential. When I learn a new program or how to post photos on Facebook I pull a muscle patting myself on the back. I've discovered a whole world of knowledge and opportunities. If I can do it, anyone can!

For those feeling technically adventurous there are free resources available online where you can learn to code in many different programming languages. It can be quite fun and challenging to create programs to advance your reach into the cyber world. You can construct your own webpage, blog, app or other online site, and manage it all by yourself, if you're so inclined.

The ironic issue about learning how to do things on a computer is that you can find out how **on your computer.** YouTube has endless tutorials on everything from **A**pple to **Z**programs. You can get in-depth instruction and learn how to do just about anything online, from fixing a leaky toilet to braiding hair. It's overwhelming, but in a good way. The opportunities are virtually endless. Just find something you're interested in and charge ahead!

Computers and smart phones are a great means to stay up to date on local events, festivals, concerts, fundraisers, the weather, and your grandchildren's school activities. Facebook, Twitter, facetime, and other social networks allow people to stay in touch with family and friends. Sites such as LinkedIn provide a platform for professionals to network. A multitude of dating sites guarantee to find your "perfect match." I should mention, from personal experience, their promise is dubious and don't believe everything that people write on their profiles. More importantly for online daters, be safe by always meeting for the first time in a public area, and let a friend know where you're going!

Banking and bill paying is a breeze when you use the online sites. Most businesses offer the option of "going paperless" which speeds the billing and payments along and helps the environment. As convenient as it is to access so many ventures online, it's important to always be alert for frauds, cons, and fake emails that implore you to reply with confidential information. Never follow a link within an email instructing you to amend your banking details, or provide your personal password. These messages are frighteningly realistic, but banks would NEVER ask you for this information so call them rather than respond to the email. When paying for an online purchase with a credit card always confirm the site address is secure. HTTP stands for "Hyper Text Transfer Protocol", and is used in the URL address for browsing websites that have no login or need to be secure. HTTPS includes **SSL** - Secure Sockets Layer, which uses encryption to keep financial data, passwords, or any sensitive information safe and secure. In addition to these cautions, it's vital to keep the security and anti-virus programs on your computer up to date, to avoid infection. Change passwords often and don't use "password" as your password. Seriously, millions of people do this!

When planning a trip you can explore endless adventures, and search for the best values on transportation, lodging and excursions. Decide in advance what you really want to do, and don't waste your time on "tourist traps" or things that don't interest you. Travel websites such as AAA, Lonely Planet and Rick Steves are valuable tools to find information about tourist sites, hotels and restaurants. Some sites like TripAdvisor have the added bonus of unbiased reviews from travelers who've been there. Unconventional travelers might enjoy the economic option of Airbnb, where you find unique lodging situations in over 190 countries. If a cruise is on your horizon, after you book a voyage, you can join a chat room of people going on the same trip. You will find great suggestions from seasoned cruisers, and the option to make plans to meet for drinks and group activities when you get onboard.

Look for local activities that you can join in. Car club activities, dog shows, beach cleanup days, art festivals, and city sponsored events that provide entertainment and great food. Some cities encourage the film industry to come to their town and shoot movies or music videos. The producers will advertise for "extras" for background and crowd scenes, and sometimes they even pay for a day's work. Wouldn't it be fun to brag about being in a movie?!

Perhaps you have an issue that is close to your heart and you want to start an online Blog, to offer advice and discuss the interest with other people on the same wavelength. Maybe you have a product or service you'd like to sell, and you can start your own website to advertise the items. Swap sites and resale opportunities are there for practically all interests. Maybe you'd like to sell some items on EBay and that could turn into a full time venture!

Even if you don't "surf the internet" on a daily basis, the computer is a valuable tool for keeping up with your photos, documents and correspondence. You can finally write that book that's been on your to-do list forever! Many people of retirement age want to write their memoirs, or their life experiences to share with their family. They don't care about being published but that might be an option too!

These suggestions for keeping your mind active are simply the tip of the iceberg. There are so many opportunities to expand your mind and keep it flexed. Whether you're a seasoned tech wiz, or a newbie, learn to utilize the gifts of the wonderful technology that's available. It's all there at the tip of your typing fingers!

Chapter 9
Embrace Your Spirituality

More than at any other point in our lives, in our retirement we contemplate our mortality and increasingly consider our spirituality. We ask ourselves those vexing questions - *Why are we here?* - *Where did we all come from?* - *Is there something bigger than us out there?* - *What is my purpose in life?* We want to resolve our minds with our thoughts on the answers, and find peace.

It used to be common for a person to be "born, raised and die" in one specific religious denomination. Traditions run deep in many families and there is nothing wrong with having firmly held beliefs that continue through a person's entire life. There is comfort in familiarity and peace in embracing an ancestor's religion.

Being a member of a congregation means you are part of a family of like-minded people. It's a place where you feel comfortable and can find harmony as you interact with others. There may be extra offerings beyond the walls of your church where you can participate in sports teams, and other community events. Churches often have groups that meet specifically for the needs of single members, seniors, or mothers who need a day off.

If you are a member of a religious community, use your retirement freedom to become more involved in your church, synagogue or house of worship. There are many opportunities for "lay persons" who want to contribute to the welfare of their congregation. Discuss your desire with your pastor or church leader to match your skills with needed tasks. Perhaps you have a lovely garden, and would like to provide some flower arrangements to enhance the church, or you enjoy teaching and would like to assist in a Sunday school class or bible study. If your talents involve organization, you can help plan a craft bazar, Christmas program, food pantry for the needy, fundraiser, or any church event that needs help. Volunteer opportunities are vast within the church community, and your contribution will always be appreciated.

As people get older, they might find that their beliefs and views have changed over the years, and an organized religion no longer suits their needs. They might have discovered that they can no longer support the strict doctrine or the demands required to maintain a membership in a church. As our world expands, we embrace the issues that are important to us. If those issues include religious dogma, such as forbidding women in the priesthood, birth control, LGBT rights, or other social situations that are in conflict with your beliefs, it's probably time to make a change. When people reach this stage, they could be drawn into a different religion that meets their current needs, or they could decide not to be involved in any organized belief system. For many, leaving a religion they've been a part of for most of their life is difficult. If possible, maintain friendships. If that's not feasible, you have to do what you believe is right.

The bottom line in determining where you stand regarding being involved in an organized religion, or choosing to move in another direction, is to **follow your heart**. As we get older (and so much wiser!), we know what we want and what we don't want. We're "over the hill" and we want our time to be spent in happiness and contentment. Coming into retirement is reason enough to evaluate our spiritual needs and make changes when we feel that's the best direction.

Just because a person leaves a religious organization doesn't mean they've become a bad person. Individuals will maintain their core beliefs, morals, ethics and values regardless of whether they go to church or not. In fact, breaking away from the constraints of a religion can produce a personal spiritual awakening. You are free to choose whatever you want to believe!

Once you are permitted to open your mind and your heart, there is a bounty of spiritual enrichment you can embrace. For instance, if you consider yourself a "Christian" perhaps you always felt a bit guilty or hesitant to accept some of the teachings of Buddhism or Taoism, or belief in other deities, like the Hindu god Ganesha, who creates the faith to remove obstacles. In retirement, there's time to research and delve into different religious teachings, to learn and make up your own mind about what you really believe. Without religious affiliation, you are now open to appreciate the lessons that speak to you, regardless of the source.

Nature is one of the most powerful ways to worship. "If you wish to know the divine, feel the wind on your face and the warm sun on your hand"(Buddha). A glorious sunrise or sunset, the view from a magnificent mountain, the ocean's waves, and the fragrance of a beautiful flower are all forms of adoration and thanks to a higher power, whoever that might be to you. Sit in the stillness of a garden, or beneath the roar of a waterfall and experience a spiritual high that you might not have ever had before. Take a hike in the forest, watch the flow of a river, witness birds and other animals in the wild. Enjoy a picnic in a scenic setting, or find a deserted area to lie on a blanket and look at the stars at night. The possibilities to gain inspiration and spiritual fulfillment from nature's bounty are endless.

Music is a spectacular way to bring joy into your life. There are times when the hard beat of a rock song keeps you moving and dancing. At other times, the music from a symphony might bring tears to your eyes, and fill you with peace. Music is so diverse, and it can produce a variety of emotions that will meet a spiritual need in your life. Take advantage of any opportunity to expand your musical preferences, such as going to an opera or a jazz performance. If you're so inclined, learn to play a musical instrument that you've always enjoyed. Music offers so many benefits and there is something for everyone to enjoy!

Spirituality can be found in the simplest things in life. The giggle of a baby, the sweet cuddle of a puppy, and the love of a good friend are events that bring a smile to our face and lightness to our soul. Embrace everything that happens in your daily life. When we were young, we didn't always have time to stop and smell the roses. Do it now! It's never too late to start appreciating all the good things this world has to offer.

A great method to have that "feel good" attitude is by looking for ways to give back, to return some of your joy to others. Find avenues to volunteer your time and talents. Depending on your skills, you might be able to join a team of charitable workers on an overseas mission, or help with a local homeless shelter. The "pay it forward" concept offers the chance to payback someone's kindness to you by being kind to someone else. Perhaps the driver ahead of you paid your fee on a toll road. You can't pay that person back, but you can pay it forward. The next time you have the opportunity, pay the toll for the driver behind you. It doesn't have to involve money and can be something as simple as helping someone with a problem, remembering how someone once helped you.

A similar idea is a "random act of kindness." Look for chance encounters that will give you the opening to do something nice, without any forethought. Say hello to a person who looks sad, buy a soda for a teenager, pick a flower and hand it to the next person you see. There are limitless ways you can show kindness when you're aware and looking for ways to spread joy. And, it's ironic that when you show kindness to others, you are rewarded by the happiness it brings!

Regardless of whether you are actively involved in a religious organization or you haven't stepped foot in a church in 50 years, there are countless means to bring a sense of worship, reverence and spirituality into your daily life. Take delight in spending time with your friends and family, enmesh yourself in nature, bask in the places you love to visit, dance to the music that makes you happy, and cloak yourself in the peace of embracing your own spirituality. There's no magic formula. It's simply what brings joy to your heart and contentment to your soul.

Chapter 10

Your Very Own Bucket List

Although the term "bucket list" was used before the movie of the same name, it became a well-known maxim after the story of two terminally ill friends decided to make a wish list of things they wanted to do before they "kicked the bucket." Viewers embraced the idea of fulfilling lifelong dreams and daring adventures when they had nothing left to lose. Here are a few items on the bucket list that these characters created.

- Witness something truly majestic
- Laugh until I cry
- Drive a Shelby Mustang
- Kiss the most beautiful girl in the world
- Get a tattoo
- Skydiving
- Spend a week at the Louvre
- See the pyramids

Everyone has something you've always wanted to do. Maybe you never had time, money, opportunity, or the courage to accomplish the fantasy. As with the above example, a wish list of things you'd like to do doesn't necessarily have to be expensive or a huge investment of your time. And, your list of challenges doesn't have to wait until you are on death's doorstep. It is simply what YOU want to do at this stage of your life.

I have a friend, who in her mid-40's, found herself at a crossroad in her life. In order to remain optimistic about her future, the idea was presented to her that she was in a position to do anything she wanted with her life. She was encouraged to think "outside the box" and imagine something she'd always dreamed of doing, but up to this point in her life circumstances had prohibited. She was free to do whatever her heart desired, and she began to brainstorm the possibilities. During several memorable vacations to Disney World, she recalled saying how much fun it would be to work there. It was a silly daydream, but the more she thought about it, the more she liked the idea. She decided it wouldn't hurt to check it out. A few weeks later, and after some basic inquiries, she was in Lake Buena Vista, Florida at the Disney World Casting Center. After an interview, was offered a role, and two weeks later she moved into an apartment near the Magic Kingdom to begin her fantasy, which lasted over ten years.

Of course, the situation I've described was a long-term experience, and a life-changing event. Not everyone is in a position to make such a drastic transformation, nor does everyone want to alter his or her entire future based on a daydream. It's simply an example of a person with an opportunity, who took a chance. It provided her with a sense of adventure and incredible happiness. By the way, when my friend left Disney World, she became a flight attendant, which was another dream on her wish list. "You are never too old to set another goal, or to dream a new dream" (C.S. Lewis).

When you get ready to make your very own bucket list, brainstorm to consider **anything and everything** that sounds intriguing to YOU. Step outside your comfort zone. If an idea makes you feel like there are butterflies in your stomach, that's something you want to write down! Get a diary or journal and make notes of your thoughts and ideas. As you begin to achieve some of the goals, write about how you feel before, during, and after the adventure. Every time I've been to a foreign country I've kept a journal, and it's exciting to read over the details years later.

As you make a list, remember the things you loved to do when you were a child, like flying a kite, or going skinny-dipping. Maybe you enjoyed riding go-carts and you can re-experience that thrill, or find a NASCAR track where they will allow you to ride along, and maybe even drive a real racecar! March in a parade, sing karaoke, and walk on a beach at sunrise, and again at sunset. Go skydiving, visit all of the US National Parks, build a treehouse, see the Seven Wonders of the World, or view the Northern Lights. Watch a ball game with your grandchildren, or visit your best friend that you haven't seen in twenty years. Your ideas can be as magnanimous as going on an expedition to Antarctica, or as humble as writing a letter to a lonely man or woman serving in the military.

If you've always wanted to travel, make plans to visit the locations that appeal to YOU, not necessarily the hot tourist spots. Check into the possibility of a "home exchange" where you swap homes with someone for a while. This is another concept made popular by a movie. *The Holiday* features two single women who swap their respective homes in England and California, and have great adventures. Airbnb is an economical option for lodging, as is Couch Surfing, although these unconventional options might not appeal to everyone.

What if you have a companion that has a different bucket list? Maybe you don't like each other's choices, or you aren't physically capable to join them on their quest. At the very least, make an attempt to share their excitement and joy. I find the idea of skydiving more frightening than fun, but if a friend wants to try it, I will be there to support them, waiting on the solid ground. On a trip to a theme park with my grandson, I vowed to ride all the roller coasters with him. The first one was smooth and fun, but the second ride was rough and bounced me around like a rag doll. I had to reconsider, and decided the rest of the day wouldn't be much fun if my grandson had to see me carted off in an ambulance. I did stay close and watched him as he enjoyed the rest of the coasters.

You might not be able to accomplish everything on your list due to health limitations or financial restrictions, but write them down anyway. Perhaps you can't climb Mount Everest, but you can live vicariously through someone else who has done it, or watch a documentary about the challenging feat. Traveling can be expensive and you might not be able to go to everyplace on your list, but you can read books and watch movies that take you on an armchair tour. My personal belief is, that we can always find a way to do the things we **really** want to do. It might take a few years to save enough money for the #1 item on your bucket list, but you can research and discover every minute detail about the adventure and look forward to the day you will fulfill your dream.

Remember, as you create and accomplish your very own bucket list, not everything has to be a spectacular challenge or expensive excursion. Often the little things in life end up being the most important. Think of the things that make you smile, thrill your soul and bring joy to your heart. That's what a bucket list is all about. "One day your life will flash before your eyes. Make sure it's worth watching"(Gerard Way).

Conclusion

I hope that the ideas I've presented in this book have been helpful in encouraging you to discover and pursue the things that make you happy in your retirement years. Start now, by writing your list of things to make it happen!

- Recognize what is most important in my life.
- Get my house in order and take care of the necessary documents for my family to follow my directives.
- Decide the best living situation for ME.
- Contemplate and plan adventures.
- Learn how to stay healthy and keep my mind active.
- Achieve the spirituality that I desire.
- Create my bucket list.
- Don't be afraid to dream a new dream each day.

Don't forget to check out the Resource section for more information and links to some of the ideas presented within the book. The best way to find out what's happening locally, and to research activities and adventures that appeal to you, is to get on the computer and search. Keep a notebook close by to write down ideas. You might add something new every day, or cross off items that you've reconsidered. Keep a daily journal to track your progress. It will be fun to read it later and see how far you've come!

Remember - There's no right or wrong! This is your journey and your time to create the retirement of your dreams. Don't be hesitant to explore different options to discover the many ways of fulfilling your vision and enjoying the life you deserve. I wish you joy and contentment as you discover what makes you happy, and leave you with some great advice. *Don't hesitate or talk about what you want to do. Just do it.* (Gbenga Akinnagbe)

Resources

The following information will clarify some of the ideas presented in the content of this book, and assist you as you research the things in YOUR life to bring you joy in your retirement years. At the time of publication, the links provided are active. The author endorses these resources for entertainment purposes, and is not associated or compensated by any business or service and makes no claim as to the content within a website.

This list is a sample of the ideas available to you, and there are hundreds more that you can find that will meet your specific needs. Look for local sites that relate to your specific location. Check your library for excellent resources, such as the "For Dummies" series that will help you learn just about anything.

sitting

Rover:
https://www.rover.com/become-a-sitter

Dogvacay:
https://dogvacay.com/how-it-works

Freelance Sites
UpWork:
https://www.upwork.com/i/howitworks/client

Guru:
http://www.guru.com/howitworks.aspx

Freelancer:
https://www.freelancer.com

Thumbtack:
https://www.thumbtack.com

Uber:
https://www.uber.com

Care Services
CareGivers:
http://www.caregivers.com

Care:
https://www.care.com

Sitter:
http://sitter.com

Chapter 2

<u>Keeping Tax Records</u>
https://www.irs.gov/Businesses/Small-Businesses-&-Self-Employed/How-long-should-I-keep-records

<u>Local sell or swap sites</u>
Ebay, Craigslist or Facebook

<u>Decluttering</u>
Spark Joy:
http://mostlovelythings.com/spark-joy-organizing
HGTV Tips:
http://www.hgtv.com/design/topics/decluttering
Zen Habits:
http://zenhabits.net/15-great-decluttering-tips
Becoming Minimalist:
http://www.becomingminimalist.com/creative-ways-to-declutter
Important Documents:
https://www.fdic.gov/news/conferences/affordable/hc achecklist.pdf

Chapter 3

Tiny Houses:
http://www.countryliving.com/home-design/g1887/tiny-house

Minimalist Living:
http://www.theminimalists.com

Chapter 4

Orient Express (Venice-Simplon):
http://www.belmond.com/venice-simplon-orient-express/luxury-trains

National Parks:
https://www.nps.gov/index.htm

Passport:
http://www.uspassportnow.com/passportapplicationservices

List of Senior Discounts:
https://onmogul.com/stories/this-list-of-senior-discounts-for-people-over-50-might-be-the-best-thing-you-learn-all-day

Chapter 5

Undiet:
http://bemorewithless.com/the-undiet

Butter vs. Margarine:
https://authoritynutrition.com/butter-vs-margarine

Portion control devices:
http://www.theportionplate.com

Chapter 6

Geocaching:
https://www.geocaching.com/play

7 Must Do Marathons:
http://running.competitor.com/2015/03/photos/7-must-5k-races-united-states_124113

Bubble Run:
http://www.bubblerun.com

Hot Chocolate Run:
https://www.hotchocolate15k.com

Rock 'n Roll Run:
http://www.runrocknroll.com

Color Run:
http://thecolorrun.com

Chapter 7

Board Games:
http://www.boardgamecentral.com/games

Card Games:
http://www.ranker.com/crowdranked-list/most-fun-card-games

Chapter 8

Learn to code:
http://websearch.about.com/od/h/g/http.htm

<u>Trip Planning</u>
TripAdvisor:
https://www.tripadvisor.com

Lonely Planet:
http://www.lonelyplanet.com

Airbnb:
https://www.airbnb.com

Movie Extras:
http://www.newfaces.com/movie-extras.php

Chapter 9

Religions of the World:
http://www.religionfacts.com

Pay it Forward:
http://thehalfwaypoint.net/2009/09/50-simple-ways-to-pay-it-forward

Random Acts of Kindness:
http://www.wikihow.com/Practice-Random-Acts-of-Kindness

Chapter 10

The Bucket List:
https://en.wikipedia.org/wiki/The_Bucket_List

The Holiday:
https://en.wikipedia.org/wiki/The_Holiday

101 Things to do before you die:
http://personalexcellence.co/blog/bucket-list-manifesto/

Write to a soldier:
http://soldiersangels.org/letter-writing-team.html

Seven Wonders:
http://geography.about.com/od/lists/a/sevenwonders.htm

Home Exchange:
https://www.homeexchange.com

Couch Surfing:
https://www.couchsurfing.com

About the Author

Find out more at oliviagreenwell.com

Olivia Greenwell, a retired hotel front desk manager, is now pursuing her long-term personal goal of becoming a published author. Residing in Tampa, Florida she enjoys spending her days going for long walks with her little dog Sammy, discovering a new love for baking, working on her writing projects and spending time with her two grand children.

Olivia's favorite thing to do is watch the sunset from the beach while reflecting on the day just spent and making plans for the next day.

Olivia is busy following her dreams in a happy retirement.

Enjoy Listening To Books?

Sign-up with Audible today and get Olivia's audiobook **So You've Retired: A Practical Guide For Your Happy Retirement** for FREE! Simply visit website **adbl.co/2mNuhSI** today.

Want A Different Book Format?

Retirement: Everything You Need To Know About Planning For And Living The Retired Life You've Always Dreamed Of is also available to purchase on Amazon in **kindle** format.

Made in the USA
Lexington, KY
15 October 2018